The Porter Principle

The Porter Principle

by
H. Byron Seymour

© Copyright 1992 — H. Byron Seymour

All rights reserved. This book is protected under the copyright laws of the United States of America. This book may not be copied or reprinted for commercial gain or profit. The use of short quotations or occasional page copying for personal or group study is permitted and encouraged. Permission will be granted upon request. Unless otherwise identified, scripture quotations are from The King James Version of the Bible.

Take note that the name satan and related names are not capitalized. We choose not to acknowledge him, even to the point of violating grammatical rules.

English definitions are from Webster's New World Dictionary, 3rd College Edition, Copyright 1988, by Simon & Schuster, Inc.

Hebrew and Greek derivatives are from Strong's Exhaustive Concordance of the Bible (with Greek and Hebrew Dictionaries), Dugan Publishers, Inc., Copyright 1890, by James Strong, Madison, N.J.

Destiny Image Publishers
P.O. Box 310
Shippensburg, PA 17257-0310

"Speaking to the Purposes of God for This Generation"

ISBN 1-56043-095-8

For Worldwide Distribution
Printed in the U.S.A.

Destiny Image books are available through these fine distributors outside the United States:

Christian Growth, Inc.,
Jalan Kilang-Timor, Singapore 0315

Successful Christian Living
Capetown, Rep. of South Africa

Lifestream
Nottingham, England

Vision Resources
Ponsonby, Auckland, New Zealand

Rhema Ministries Trading
Randburg, South Africa

WA Buchanan Company
Geebung, Queensland, Australia

Salvation Book Centre
Petaling, Jaya, Malaysia

Word Alive
Niverville, Manitoba, Canada

Contents

Chapter		Page
	Acknowledgments	vii
	Foreword	ix
	Introduction	xi
	Other Materials by Pastor Seymour	xv
1	Heavenly and Earthly Porters	1
2	The Order of Porters	13
3	How the Thief Gains Access	25
4	Adam, Porter of the Garden	37
5	The Importance of a Church Home	53
6	The Danger of Relinquishing Control to Satan	67
7	Recognizing and Avoiding Dangerous Influences	79
8	The Bishop Ministry	89
9	Restoring the Bishop Ministry	105
10	Taming the Wild Ass	115
11	The Porter Inside You	123
12	The Struggle Within	131
13	I Will Stand Upon My Watch	139

Acknowledgments

I gratefully and sincerely acknowledge:

God, my Sovereign, who is the original source of all spiritual truths; Him, I love with my very life.

My parents, who brought me into this world. For the sure spiritual foundation my Dad laid in me from a child, I deeply love.

My beloved children, Jody and Jenifer and for my deceased wife Gloria, who have so faithfully stood by my side and have so willingly understood God's purposes; them, I deeply love with my life.

My wonderful church family at Church Of The Sovereign God, who cleave to and help me so faithfully, who understand my God-given commission that extends beyond the region where we assemble; I truly love and appreciate them.

My typing and editing assistant, Stacia, who worked so diligently transcribing my tapes and helping to put this in manuscript form; I thank her.

The financial contributors; Donald and Sarah who contributed the most, and for all those in my church and for all the others who made this book financially possible, I gratefully love and thank you—may God bless and prosper you.

The different men of God, from whom I have received nuggets and seeds that have helped me in the compiling of this principle, to them I am eternally grateful.

Foreword

The vital truths in this book on "The Porter Principle" touch every area of the Christian life today. Never before have we so urgently needed the important work of the biblical "porter," or doorkeeper.

As I travel across the United States and minister overseas, I recognize that a great deal of our personal and ministerial pain and suffering could be avoided if godly *porters* stood at the gate of our homes, churches and nations.

When individual believers begin to "porter" their own lives, carefully regulating what goes in and what comes out of their inner beings, they will be transformed. They will affect everyone and everything they touch and relate to! Wasn't that our Lord's intention when He said we were to be the salt of the world?

Byron Seymour is my precious friend, and for that I would gladly have foreworded this book, but as I studied the context of the manuscript, I realized that this powerful message must be spoken to all of us. Byron was thorough, as usual.

He didn't leave any of us out...he clearly shows us from God's Word that we are all to function as porters in our own lives to protect the issues of our hearts. He shows how the functions of the porter as leader, protector and corrector in the family unit are vital to the spiritual and physical health and safety of our families.

Byron Seymour then reveals the importance of the neglected and misunderstood role of the spiritual office of the porter in the Church—referred to in Scripture as the bishop and the apostle.

This book is the forerunner to the message of "order and alignment." It comes in the spirit of Elijah, John the Baptist and Jesus. In this writing the spirit of man finds its par. Thank God for this revelation. It is destined to play a key role in God's plan for the supernatural destiny of the Church in our day. May we all be doers of this word, and not hearers only.

Dr. Mark Hanby
October 1992

Introduction

When we use the term "porter" these days, we usually think of *a person who carries things* or a *railroad employee who waits on passengers in a parlor car or sleeper.* There is, however, an older use of the word, one the Bible uses on a number of occasions in both the Old and New Testaments. It means: *one who has the charge of a door or gate; a doorman; a gatekeeper.* While the King James Version of the Bible uses *porter* or *keeper*, other versions translate the original as *gatekeeper, doorkeeper, keeper, watchman* or simply *the one at the door.*

At first glance, we might not think that a person charged with watching a door has a very important position. But just the opposite is true. A porter, in Bible times, was entrusted with the safety and well-being of entire cities. Therefore he had to be a very mature and responsible person.

David set porters over the entrance of his Tabernacle, the place where the presence of God rested, over the treasury of the Tabernacle and over the doors of his own palace. These appointed men were so important that they were listed with the priests and the singers.

And the PORTERS were, Shallum, and Akkub, and Talmon, and Ahiman, and their brethren: Shallum was the chief;

I Chronicles 9:17

All these which were chosen to be PORTERS in the gates were two hundred and twelve. These were reckoned by their genealogy in their villages, whom David and Samuel the seer did ordain in their set office.

I Chronicles 9:22

For these Levites, the four chief PORTERS, were in their set office, and were over the chambers and treasuries of the house of God.

I Chronicles 9:26

At one point, David had 4000 porters.

Moreover four thousand were PORTERS; and four thousand praised the Lord with the instruments which I made, said David, to praise therewith.

I Chronicles 23:5

When Solomon built the first Temple in Jerusalem, he followed the orders of his father and placed porters to guard the entrances of the new edifice.

And he appointed, according to the order of David his father, the courses of the priests to their service, and the Levites to their charges, to praise and minister before the priests, as the duty of every day required: the PORTERS also by their courses at every gate: for so had David the man of God commanded.

II Chronicles 8:14

Fully one-third of the Levites were assigned to this important duty.

This is the thing that ye shall do; A third part of you entering on the sabbath, of the priests and of the Levites, shall be PORTERS of the doors;

II Chronicles 23:4

What were these porters guarding against? They were guarding against unauthorized entry, and they were guarding against uncleanness.

And he set the PORTERS at the gates of the house of the Lord, that none which was unclean in any thing should enter in.

II Chronicles 23:19

When Nehemiah returned to Judah from captivity and rebuilt the walls and restored the gates of the Holy City, he immediately appointed porters to guard those gates.

Now it came to pass, when the wall was built, and I had set up the doors, and the PORTERS and the singers and Levites were appointed,

Nehemiah 7:1

The PORTERS: the children of Shallum, the children of Ater, the children of Talmon, the children of Akkub, the children of Hatita, the children of Shobai, an hundred thirty and eight.

Nehemiah 7:45

The people of Israel supported the porters, just as they did the priests and other Levites, recognizing their importance to the welfare of everyone concerned.

And all Israel in the days of Zerubbabel, and in the days of Nehemiah, gave the portions of the singers and the PORTERS, every day his portion: and they sanctified holy things unto the Levites; and the Levites sanctified them unto the children of Aaron.

Nehemiah 12:47

And he had prepared for him a great chamber, where aforetime they laid the meat offerings, the frankincense, and the vessels, and the tithes of the corn, the new wine, and the oil, which was commanded to be given to the Levites, and the singers, and the PORTERS; and the offerings of the priests.

Nehemiah 13:5

Just as the older meaning of the word *porter* has been practically lost today, the service performed by these godly men is tragically missing from the Church at the close of the twentieth century. It is rare to find these days those who are willing and able to accept the responsibility of guarding and watching over the spiritual welfare of others.

God intended for porters to guard our church assemblages, our souls, and our families, to shelter us with their covering. In this way, we can be fastened in surety and hedged about in defense. This can come about only as we learn God's order for our lives and submit ourselves to that order. When the Body is in direct and proper alignment, the Lord is able to pour His anointing and revelation upon us, and it flows to every part. This is God's will for His Church. This is *the porter principle*.

Other Materials Available from *H. Byron Seymour*

Teaching/Training Manuals

WHAT IT TAKES TO BECOME A MAN/WOMAN OF GOD $12.00

MEET FOR THE MASTER'S USE: To Know What Is In Your Heart: 30 Fold Level $12.00

MEET FOR THE MASTER'S USE: Greater Maturity And Authority By Overcoming Satan's Testing: 60 Fold Level; Losing The Self-Life: 100 Fold Level $12.00

REBUILDING FAITH AND CONFIDENCE AFTER TESTING AND MINISTRY PREPARATION $12.00

Other Books

PATHWAYS TO HEALING	$2.00
TOTAL HEALING FOR YOU	$3.00

Audio Cassette Series

THE TRY OF DESTINY	$30.00
COME TO ME ELISHA	$25.00
THE RETURN OF THE RULE OF GOD	$40.00
THE JORDAN EXPERIENCE	$25.00
THE WEAVINGS OF GOD	$35.00
GOD'S EARTHLY UTOPIA	$45.00
THE CALL OF THE APOSTLE	$45.00
GOD'S SECRET CHAMBERS	$45.00

**Send your orders to:
H. Byron Seymour
P.O. Box 33127
Raleigh, NC 27636-3127**

Chapter 1

Heavenly and Earthly Porters

And He said unto them, I beheld Satan as lightning fall from heaven.

Luke 10:18

Long before God created man, He created angelic beings. When He laid the foundations of the earth, angels were already present.

Where wast thou when I laid the foundations of the earth? declare, if thou hast understanding. Who hath laid the measures thereof, if thou knowest? or who hath stretched the line upon it? Whereupon are the foundations thereof fastened? or who laid the corner stone thereof; When the morning stars sang together, and all the sons of God shouted for joy?

Job 38:4-7

These *sons of God* were angels. The Hebrew word translated *morning stars* means *princes or stars who kneel or* bless, salute, praise, and congratulate God. Angels were created for God's praise. Lucifer was one of the most powerful and beautiful of them all.

> *Thus saith the Lord God; Thou sealest up the sum, full of wisdom, and perfect in beauty. Thou hast been in Eden the garden of God; every precious stone was thy covering, the sardius, topaz, and the diamond, the beryl, the onyx, and the jasper, the sapphire, the emerald, and the carbuncle, and gold: the workmanship of thy tabrets and of thy pipes was prepared in thee in the day that thou wast created. Thou art the anointed cherub that covereth; and I have set thee so: thou wast upon the holy mountain of God; thou hast walked up and down in the midst of the stones of fire. Thou wast perfect in thy ways from the day that thou wast created, till iniquity was found in thee.*
>
> Ezekiel 28:12-15

Lucifer was not an ordinary angel. He ranked with Michael and Gabriel as an archangel or leader among the hosts of angelic beings. Yet he was not satisfied. He wanted to be equal to God. He rebelled against God and, as a result, was thrust out of Heaven.

> *How art thou fallen from heaven, O Lucifer, son of the morning! how art thou cut down to the ground, which didst weaken the nations! For thou hast said in thine heart, I will ascend into heaven, I will exalt my throne above the stars of God: I will sit also upon the mount of the congregation, in the sides of the north: I will ascend above the heights of the clouds; I will be like the most High.*
>
> Isaiah 14:12-14

Determined to *ascend above the stars of God,* determined to be *like the most High,* lucifer rebelled against God. He thus became the enemy of God and man and was exiled from the presence of the Creator.

Yet thou shalt be brought down to hell, to the sides of the pit.

Isaiah 14:15

Through his rebellion, satan lost his authority and began his attempt to seduce the nations. He tries to appear as an angel of light, the opposite of what he really is. He structures his principalities to look just like the apostles of God, the exact opposite of what they really are. Just as the anti-christ (if there is a literal man as the anti-christ) will one day sit in the temple of God, satan desires to enter and rule in those of us who are the temple of God.

When satan entered into Judas (see John 13:27), this same spirit of rebelliousness came upon him, and he set about to betray Jesus. As a result, Judas lost his place at Jesus' side. David foresaw prophetically the curses which would come upon those who betrayed and crucified the Savior.

Let their habitation be desolate; and let none dwell in their tents. For they persecute him whom Thou hast smitten; and they talk to the grief of those whom Thou hast wounded. Add iniquity unto their iniquity: and let them not come into Thy righteousness. Let them be blotted out of the book of the living, and not be written with the righteous.

Psalm 69:25-28

When the disciples were looking for a replacement for Judas, this Psalm was quoted.

For he was numbered with us, and had obtained part of this ministry. Now this man purchased a field with the reward of iniquity; and falling headlong, he burst asunder in the midst, and all his bowels gushed out. And it was known unto all the dwellers at Jerusalem; insomuch as that field is called in their proper tongue, Aceldama, that is to say, The field of blood. For it is written in the book of Psalms, Let his habitation be desolate, and let no man dwell therein: and his bishoprick let another take.

Acts 1:17-20

Judas was destined to be a bishop among men, just as lucifer held the position of bishop in Heaven. When each of them fell, they were replaced.

When lucifer revolted, he coerced a third of the angels to join him.

And his tail drew the third part of the stars of heaven, and did cast them to the earth:

Revelation 12:4

Now, as satan, lucifer is dedicated to deceiving as many men and women as he can to follow him to ruin. One day all nations will see him for what he really is.

They that see thee shall narrowly look upon thee, and consider thee, saying, Is this the man that made the earth to tremble, that did shake kingdoms; that made the world as a wilderness, and destroyed the cities thereof; that opened not the house of his prisoners?

Isaiah 14:16-17

The important thing to remember here is that satan could not prevail against the throne of God and that Jesus actually

Heavenly and Earthly Porters 5

watched while the rebel was thrown down. He said, *"I beheld satan as lightning fall from heaven"* (Luke 10:18). God didn't have to lift a finger against the rebellious lucifer. He had faithful heavenly porters who guarded His gates against evil. Those porters did their job well. Lucifer never made it to the throne room of God. The porters kept him out.

Jesus watched it happen. He saw His faithful servants performing their assigned tasks, throwing satan out of Heaven as fast as lightning falls.

What mighty beings angels are! There is an account of atheistic Russian cosmonauts seeing huge angelic beings, each the size of a jumbo jet, in outer space. I believe it. Angels are enormous and powerful!

When lucifer and his angels tried to take over God's Kingdom, they encountered great resistance. They were met by the heavenly warlords, led by Michael (*Michael* means *Who is like God?*). The rebels didn't have a chance against these forces.

> *And there was war in heaven: Michael and his angels fought against the dragon; and the dragon fought and his angels, and prevailed not; neither was their place found any more in heaven. And the great dragon was cast out, that old serpent, called the devil, and satan, which deceiveth the whole world: he was cast out into the earth, and his angels were cast out with him.*
>
> Revelation 12:7-9

There is no place in the presence of God for rebels. Michael and his aides simply lifted their wings and said to lucifer, "You may not enter here. There is no place here for your kind." That day Michael proved that no one can be like God.

Michael prevailed. He remained in the presence of God, but lucifer had to go. The rebellious departed, and the faithful remained. God had faithful porters around His throne. Satan could not get close enough to touch it. He was unceremoniously kicked out the gate.

With the fall of lucifer our own struggles began. Satan, seeing that he was powerless against the forces of Heaven, and bitter, for having failed in his attempt to overthrow God, set his attention upon the earth and the creature made in God's image. If he could not hurt God directly, he would work to deceive God's companions, man and woman. Thus began our constant battle with him.

For we wrestle not against flesh and blood, but against principalities, against powers, against the rulers of the darkness of this world, against spiritual wickedness in high places.

Ephesians 6:12

Satan and his legions work to block the will of God in our lives. For example, only the direct intervention of Michael enabled Daniel to receive a message satan had opposed.

Then said he unto me, Fear not, Daniel: for from the first day that thou didst set thine heart to understand, and to chasten thyself before thy God, thy words were heard, and I am come for thy words. But the prince of the kingdom of Persia withstood me one and twenty days: but, lo, Michael, one of the chief princes, came to help me; and I remained there with the kings of Persia. Now I am come to make thee

understand what shall befall thy people in the latter days: for yet the vision is for many days.
Daniel 10:12-14

Jesus took it upon Himself to be the Porter to the presence of God, the Doorkeeper to salvation. He said:

I am the way, the truth, and the life: no man cometh unto the Father, but by Me.
John 14:6

When He came to earth in human form, as the God-Man, Jesus opposed satan on every front and left us an example to follow.

How God anointed Jesus of Nazareth with the Holy Ghost and with power: who went about doing good, and healing all that were oppressed of the devil; for God was with Him.
Acts 10:38

Now that the theater of battle has shifted to the earth, God prefers to use men as His porters, not angels, even though angels are still assigned by God to protect God's people. But, just as Jesus could stand against the enemy only because *God was with Him*, we cannot oppose satan or his legions on our own. God, through His five-fold ministry, is building us up so He can defeat and stop the devil through His born-again man.

God delights in using people, in demonstrating His power through us. When He desired to heal the lame man at the Beautiful gate, He used Peter to do it.

Then Peter said, Silver and gold have I none; but such as I have give I thee: In the name of Jesus Christ of Nazareth rise up and walk. And he took him by the right hand, and lifted him up: and immediately his feet and ankle bones received strength. And he leaping up stood, and walked, and entered with them into the temple, walking, and leaping, and praising God. And all the people saw him walking and praising God:

Acts 3:6-9

Peter was so infused with the power of God that even his shadow would heal people as he passed by them.

Insomuch that they brought forth the sick into the streets, and laid them on beds and couches, that at the least the shadow of Peter passing by might overshadow some of them. There came also a multitude out of the cities round about unto Jerusalem, bringing sick folks, and them which were vexed with unclean spirits: and they were healed every one.

Acts 5:15-16

The apostle Paul was used of God in a similar way. When a sorcerer named Barjesus tried to impede the gospel Paul preached, he was struck blind.

And when they had gone through the isle unto Paphos, they found a certain sorcerer, a false prophet, a Jew, whose name was Barjesus: which was with the deputy of the country, Sergius Paulus, a prudent man; who called for Barnabas and Saul, and desired to hear the word of God. But Elymas the sorcerer (for so is his name by interpretation) withstood them, seeking to turn away the deputy from the faith. Then Saul, (who also is called Paul,) filled with the Holy Ghost, set his eyes on him, and said, O full of all subtilty and all mischief, thou child of the devil, thou enemy

of all righteousness, wilt thou not cease to pervert the right ways of the Lord? And now, behold, the hand of the Lord is upon thee, and thou shalt be blind, not seeing the sun for a season. And immediately there fell on him a mist and a darkness; and he went about seeking some to lead him by the hand. Then the deputy, when he saw what was done, believed, being astonished at the doctrine of the Lord.
Acts 13:6-12

When Paul was confronted with the damsel who had a spirit of divination, he took control of the situation.

And it came to pass, as we went to prayer, a certain damsel possessed with a spirit of divination met us, which brought her masters much gain by soothsaying: the same followed Paul and us, and cried, saying, These men are the servants of the most high God, which shew unto us the way of salvation. And this did she many days. But Paul, being grieved, turned and said to the spirit, I command thee in the name of Jesus Christ to come out of her. And he came out the same hour.
Acts 16:16-18

Jesus chose men to follow in His footsteps, to stand guard over His flock against the evil attacks of our common enemy. God appointed His porters on the earth. He placed mature leadership to porter the Church. We have come to call those positions of leadership "the five-fold ministry": apostles, prophets, evangelists, pastors and teachers.

And He gave some, apostles; and some, prophets; and some, evangelists; and some, pastors and teachers;
Ephesians 4:11

The apostle Paul places these five offices in order of their need to the Church.

> *And God hath set some in the church, first apostles, secondarily prophets, thirdly teachers, after that...*
>
> I Corinthians 12:28

Then would come the pastors and evangelist. This means that God first must set foundational governing and order, then guidance, then grounding and purpose in your life, then you need a pastor to guard and care for the flock, and then an evangelist to gather the lost into a house of God that can guard, ground, guide and govern God's people. This order will cause them to be portered correctly.

In His Word, He made clear the reasons for placing such leadership in the Church.

> *For the perfecting of the saints, for the work of the ministry, for the edifying of the body of Christ: till we all come in the unity of the faith, and of the knowledge of the Son of God, unto a perfect man, unto the measure of the stature of the fulness of Christ: that we henceforth be no more children, tossed to and fro, and carried about with every wind of doctrine, by the sleight of men, and cunning craftiness, whereby they lie in wait to deceive; but speaking the truth in love, may grow up into him in all things, which is the head, even Christ: from whom the whole body fitly joined together and compacted by that which every joint supplieth, according to the effectual working in the measure of every part, maketh increase of the body unto the edifying of itself in love.*
>
> Ephesians 4:12-16

God's five-fold ministry is to train God's people to know how to generally porter their lives. Every Christian is to mature into a general porter of his or her life. As such, we are often satan's target. I have personally experienced the opposition of hell. When I first came to Raleigh in 1987, God told me that the principality that answers directly to satan in that region had all his guns aimed at me, to destroy me. Satan's forces unleashed severe attacks and strategy against my life and ministry. But if we are secure in God, we have nothing to fear. Satan cannot defeat God. God continues to foil the plans of satan, using His people to demonstrate His might and wisdom to the universe!

Lucifer could not prevail against the throne of God, and one day he will no longer be able to prevail against the Church. God has promised to build His Church in thoroughness and completeness.

Upon this rock I will build My church; and the gates of hell shall not prevail against it.

Matthew 16:18

That word *build* means *to plan, to structure, to construct, and to confirm*. The building God puts together will be totally stable and firm. First, God makes His plans. Then He lays the proper foundations. He then builds on those foundations. Finally, He will confirm and finish His work. Christ has not come simply to get the lost into Heaven; He has come to bring total salvation for the total man. This is a process of maturing, of coming into order. And it is a lifelong operation.

When we pray: *"Thy kingdom come,"* we are asking for His Kingdom *to appear, to enter, to grow, and to be set*. And we were taught to pray that this would be done *in earth as it is in heaven* (Matthew 6:10). What is taking place in Heaven should be taking place here on the earth. God's will is being done in Heaven. We must allow it to be done on the earth, as well. And we must continue to allow His will to be done here until we get things *down here* in order as He has them *up there*. When that day comes, the gates of hell will no longer be able to prevail. Satan will no longer be able to bring discouragement, disappointment, and defeat. God's final goal, that of having His Kingdom here on earth in its completeness, with us, will be realized.

We can hasten that day by learning the secrets of *the porter principle*.

Chapter 2

The Order of Porters

Obey them that have the rule over you, and submit yourselves: for they watch for your souls, as they that must give account, that they may do it with joy, and not with grief: for that is unprofitable for you.

Hebrews 13:17

The Church needs porters, those who guard us against evil, at every level of our lives. We need porters as individuals; we need porters in the home; and we need porters in the Church. God has made provision for these various levels of mature leadership. And, if the Church is willing to follow His will, He will cause our to be set in the proper order, so that we can be guarded vigilantly against the designs of the enemy upon our lives.

When God is moving in the church, the individual and the home, His life will affect the community in which you live, as well as the state, the nation, and the world. But the effect on these larger areas begins with order in the Church and order in the home. The example for the individual and the family must also come from the Church. If the Church is not in order, how can the home be in order? If the Church is not in order, how can the individual be in order? True order must begin with the Church. If the Church is not in order, how can we blame the world for what happens around us? Peter wrote to the churches, saying:

Judgment must begin at the house of God:

1 Peter 4:17

Jesus will not return to a Church in disorder. God will not give us the Promised Land until we yield ourselves completely to His will for our lives. When God is in complete control, then He can manifest His power in the Church, saving the lost *en masse*, performing healings and miracles, and bringing revelation. His power can then be felt in the entire world. *The porter principle* requires order, God's order.

All order begins with Jesus. He is the Way, the Truth and the Life. He is the Door of the Sheepfold.

I am the door of the sheep.

John 10:7

Under Jesus, the Shepherd and Bishop of our souls, we need godly men and women who will stand as porters at the gates, to keep out what God wants kept out and to let in what God wants in. These must be vigilant and wise people; for satan never rests. He is a constant threat to the Sheepfold.

These porters will have the authority to open or close the door to demonic activity in the Church, in the family, and in the life of an individual. This is serious business that demands diligence.

The Order of Porters 15

Satan is a thief. A thief takes what legally belongs to someone else. If allowed to have his way, satan will systematically devastate your church, cheat your family of its heritage, and rob you as a person. His goal is to pull down the Kingdom of God in your church, in your family, in you, in your region, in your nation, and in the whole world. He will do it—if you let him get away with it. Proper porterage will stop satan's strategy to do such.

There is, however, no reason for him to have victory. Christ has *redeemed us from the curse.*

Christ hath redeemed us from the curse of the law, being made a curse for us: for it is written, Cursed is every one that hangeth on a tree:
Galatians 3:13

He has established the leadership of the Church to aid the Church in the battle and to keep safe what He has purchased with His own sacrifice.

Jesus recognized the importance of the porter. He likened Himself to a man who went on a journey, but who left responsible servants to care for his interests at home.

For the Son of man is as a man taking a far journey, who left his house, and gave authority to his servants, and to every man his work, and commanded the porter to watch.
Mark 13:34

He said that a porter should be able to recognize the true Shepherd and to open to Him.

But he that entereth in by the door is the shepherd of the sheep. To him the porter openeth; and the sheep hear his voice: and he calleth his own sheep by name, and leadeth them out.

John 10:2-3

When Moses was about to die, he saw the need for a serious man to take the position of a spiritual porter over the people of Israel. Joshua became that man.

And Moses spake unto the Lord, saying, Let the Lord, the God of the spirits of all flesh, SET a man over the congregation, which may go out before them, and which may go in before them, and which may lead them out, and which may bring them in; that the congregation of the Lord be not as sheep which have no shepherd.

Numbers 27:15-17

As we have seen, this is still God's method of guarding His people in the New Testament.

And God hath SET some in the church, first apostles, secondarily prophets, thirdly teachers, after that miracles, then gifts of healings, helps, governments, diversities of tongues.

I Corinthians 12:28

After the governing and the proper setting of things in order by the apostle, the guiding voice of the prophet, and the proper grounding of the teacher, God also sets pastors and evangelists to help porter His flock. The use of this term *set* in both the Old and New Testaments led Dr. Mark Hanby some years ago to coin the phrase "set-man," when referring to a person God chooses and places over His flock to guard it against the evil intentions of the enemy. God's set-man is a porter, a bishop, a shepherd over those people. As such, the set-man is responsible to God for the oversight of those entrusted to his care. A set-man can be any of the five-fold ministry gifts. A set-man, regardless of doma five-fold gift office will have shepherding ability. This goes along with God setting a man over the congregation. An evangelist is the least likely, but can be a set-man if God so deems. Helping the set-man to do his job well, there may be under-shepherds, under-bishops. These must also be serious and dedicated watchmen.

> *Son of man, I have made thee a watchman unto the house of Israel: therefore hear the Word at My mouth, and give them warning from Me.*
>
> Ezekiel 3:17

The Hebrew word translated *watchman* is *tsaphah*, meaning *to lean forward to peer into the distance, to observe or await, to behold, espy, to look up, and to keep the watch.* Watchmen, who are the leaders in any body of Christ, report to the set-porter, thus establishing a complete system of vigilant oversight for the Church.

> *And David sat between the two gates: and the watchman went up to the roof over the gate unto the wall, and lifted up his eyes, and looked, and behold a man running alone. And the watchman cried, and told the king. And the king said, If he be alone, there is tidings in his mouth. And he came apace, and drew near. And the watchman saw another man running: and the watchman called unto the porter, and said, Behold another man running alone. And the king said, He also bringeth tidings.*
>
> II Samuel 18:24-26

In this case, the watchman reported everything to the king and to the porter. The watchman was alert. He saw a runner approaching long before that runner reached the gates. The job of the watchman was to report what he saw to a higher authority. This particular watchman was faithful to do that. He recognized the correct order.

> *Take heed therefore unto yourselves, and to all the flock, over which the Holy Ghost hath made you overseers, to feed the church of God.*
>
> Acts 20:28

God's set-man has the oversight, portership, and bishoprick of your soul. The word *soul* here is *psuche* which is your mind, emotions and will. This is the psychological/self man. This is the realm or arena where man is stubborn, rebellious and in error. Most of us don't even realize we have a problem there. Jesus owns your spirit but calls men of God to have the oversight of your soul. Your destiny is entrusted to godly and God-ordained men. Your responsibility is to submit yourself to the person God has placed over you. Follow him as a trusted guide. He is accountable to God and will answer to Him for the counsel he gives you. Your set-man's oversight comes from the Word of God. They take the oversight of your soul with the Word of God.

> *Obey them that have the rule over you, and submit yourselves, for they watch for your souls, as they that must give account, that they may do it with joy and not with grief.*
>
> Hebrews 13:17

This phrase, *have the rule over you*, also implies *being the guide, giving guidance.* The word for *watch* is *agrupuneo*, which means *to be sleepless and to keep awake.* Our porters are to lead us, to drive us or to carry us, whichever is necessary. They must watch over and guide the lives of others, denying themselves and their own wishes in order to accomplish it. They must have the good of others as their first and foremost concern. What a great responsibility! The Church is not to complicate the job of the set-men by resisting their authority. The Church's humble submission to their authority will allow them to do their assigned task with joy.

One of the most difficult tasks of the set-man is to keep unity of his God-given commission and among God's people who carry it out in the Body of Christ. Satan never ceases to try to draw the individual believer away from his set-man and his fellow believers. The apostle Paul, a chosen porter of the first century, cried out for unity.

> *I therefore, the prisoner of the Lord, beseech you that ye walk worthy of the vocation wherewith ye are called, with all lowliness and meekness, with longsuffering, forbearing one another in love; endeavouring to keep the unity of the Spirit in the bond of peace.*
>
> Ephesians 4:1-3

He went on to show that the way to achieve unity was for each of us to submit to the authority of the five-fold ministry (See verses 8-16).

Because set-men are chosen and assigned by God to care for your souls, you should love and respect them under God Himself. We should depend on those who are set over us. These are your God-assigned representatives, shepherds or porters.

One very poignant biblical example is the reaction of the Ephesian believers, when Paul had finished his farewell discourse, and they thought they might never see him again.

> *And when he had thus spoken, he kneeled down, and prayed with them all. And they all wept sore, and fell on Paul's neck, and kissed him, sorrowing most of all for the*

words which he spake, that they should see his face no more. And they accompanied him unto the ship.

Acts 20:36-38

God has given a vision and a commission to the men He has entrusted with the gates of the Church. We should love that vision and be in agreement with it. It is of God. The apostle Paul enjoined the Corinthian believers to do just that.

Now I beseech you, brethren, by the name of our Lord Jesus Christ, that ye all speak the same thing, and that there be no divisions among you; but that ye be perfectly joined together in the same mind and in the same judgment.

I Corinthians 1:10

Love and unity are important not only with those who are set over the Church, but also with one another. God never intended that His people split off into cliques. He desires one undivided family. The writer to the Hebrews likewise urged unity.

Let brotherly love continue.

Hebrews 13:1

Jesus had made this loving unity both a command and a test of true discipleship.

A new commandment I give unto you, That ye love one another; as I have loved you, that ye also love one another. By this shall all men know that ye are My disciples, if ye have love one to another.

John 13:34-35

To the Ephesians, the apostle Paul summarized the correct order of *the porter principle*, through which He can manifest His power on our behalf.

Now therefore ye are no more strangers and foreigners, but fellow-citizens with the saints, and of the household of God; and are built on the foundation of the apostles and prophets, Jesus Christ Himself being the chief corner stone; in whom all the building fitly framed together groweth into an holy temple in the Lord: in whom ye also are builded together for an habitation of God through the Spirit.
Ephesians 2:19-22

That Christ may dwell in your hearts by faith; that ye, being rooted and grounded in love, may be able to comprehend with all saints what is the breadth, and length, and depth, and height; and to know the love of Christ, which passeth knowledge, that ye might be filled with all the fulness of God. Now unto Him that is able to do exceeding abundantly above all that we ask or think, according to the power that worketh in us, unto Him be glory in the church by Christ Jesus throughout all ages, world without end. Amen.
Ephesians 3:17-21

Christ is the Head. He has set men in positions of authority as earthly porters. Others are set under these porters as sub-shepherds. This leadership was not intended as an imposition upon the believers. We are the intended beneficiaries of God's loving order. For this reason, we willingly and joyfully submit to God and to His men.

Jesus left us a powerful example. He did nothing apart from His Father.

Jesus answered them, and said, My doctrine is not Mine, but His that sent Me. If any man will do His will, he shall know of the doctrine, whether it be of God, or whether I speak of Myself. He that speaketh of himself seeketh his own glory: but He that seeketh His glory that sent Him, the same is true, and no unrighteousness is in Him.

John 7:16-18

Then cried Jesus in the temple as He taught, saying, Ye both know Me, and ye know whence I am: and I am not come of Myself, but He that sent Me is true, whom ye know not.

John 7:28

Then said Jesus unto them, When ye have lifted up the Son of man, then shall ye know that I am He, and that I do nothing of Myself; but as My Father hath taught Me, I speak these things.

John 8:28

There are many other references to the same truth. Jesus did nothing of Himself. He was fully submitted to the Father and *His* will. Everything He did was motivated by what His Father told Him to do, and He recognized Father God as His HEAD.

...the head of Christ is God.

I Corinthians 11:3

Because the Father was His HEAD, Jesus spent much time in prayer, receiving instruction for His life and ministry, instruction from above.

And when He had sent the multitudes away, He went up into a mountain apart to pray: and when the evening was come, He was there alone.

Matthew 14:23

And in the morning, rising up a great while before day, He went out, and departed into a solitary place, and there prayed.
Mark 1:35

And He withdrew Himself into the wilderness, and prayed.
Luke 5:16

And it came to pass in those days, that He went out into a mountain to pray, and continued all night in prayer to God.
Luke 6:12

Then answered Jesus and said unto them, Verily, verily, I say unto you, The Son can do nothing of Himself, but what He seeth the Father do: for what things soever He doeth, these also doeth the Son likewise.
John 5:19

I can of Mine own self do nothing: as I hear, I judge: and My judgment is just; because I seek not Mine own will, but the will of the Father which hath sent Me.
John 5:30

The prime example of Jesus' submission to the will of the Father is found in His prayer in the Garden of Gethsemane.

And He went a little further, and fell on His face, and prayed, saying, O My Father, if it be possible, let this cup pass from Me: nevertheless not as I will, but as Thou wilt.
Matthew 26:39

If Jesus believed that order was sufficiently important that He did nothing and said nothing of Himself, surely we can submit to the order God has ordained for each of us—for the purpose of receiving the greater good.

There is also a proper order for the family. We shall discuss that proper order in Chapter 4, as we continue to explore the truths of *the porter principle*.

Chapter 3

How the Thief Gains Access

Verily, verily, I say unto you, He that entereth not by the door into the sheepfold, but climbeth up some other way, the same is a thief and a robber.

John 10:1

This is a perfect description of satan. He loves to climb up *some other way* and try to bypass the porters God has placed to faithfully guard the doors. The word for *climb* means *arise, ascend, and go up,* and it comes from a root word meaning *severity, repetition, and intensity.* Satan is persistent in his attempts to get a foothold somewhere, somehow. He is a thief and a robber. He breaks in where he has no right to be. His desire is to steal, kill, and destroy.

The thief cometh not, but for to steal, and to kill, and to destroy:

John 10:10

Satan will filch anything he can get his hands on. He will rush in to immolate, to slaughter, and to leave in utter chaos any unprotected life. He doesn't want you to progress and is intent on your destruction. He is the opposite of all that Jesus is; and he does the opposite of all that Jesus does.

Satan is forever trying to take from you something that God has already given you. If there is anyway that he can successfully pull it away from you, he will.

His greatest tool is deception. He has mastered the art.

Ye are of your father the devil, and the lusts of your father ye will do. He was a murderer from the beginning, and abode not in the truth, because there is no truth in him. When he speaketh a lie, he speaketh of his own: for he is a liar, and the father of it.

John 8:44

The soul of man is susceptible to deceit. It was this satanic power to deceive that turned the heads of Adam and Eve from the One who had given them life to an impostor who could not make good on his claims to make them *as gods*.

For God doth know that in the day ye eat thereof, then your eyes shall be opened, and ye shall be as gods, knowing good and evil.

Genesis 3:5

When we speak of the soul of man, the *psuche*, we are speaking of *the mind, emotions and will*. This is the area of man that becomes the stronghold of satan. He has the ability to deceive and charm. When a person is sufficiently charmed, satan can walk right in without a fight.

Even Christians are subject to deceit. We must remember that the spirit of anti-christ is in the world. Some *perish because they receive not the love of the truth*.

How the Thief Gains Access 27

And then shall that Wicked be revealed, whom the Lord shall consume with the spirit of His mouth, and shall destroy with the brightness of His coming: even him, whose coming is after the working of Satan with all power and signs and lying wonders, and with all deceivableness of unrighteousness in them that perish; because they received not the love of the truth, that they might be saved. And for this cause God shall send them strong delusion, that they should believe a lie: that they all might be damned who believed not the truth, but had pleasure in unrighteousness.
II Thessalonians 2:8-12

As happened with our fathers, Adam and Eve, God may allow some Christians to be deceived, at least for a season, until they come to their senses.

The satanic lies most often believed by Christians are interesting. One of the most common is a play on our pride, making us think that we are more than we actually are. The image we get of our importance to God (and of what we will do in the future for Him) causes many to stumble and to run ahead of those who are advising them spiritually. If satan can cause us to jump ahead and to take on tasks for which we are not yet prepared, he can easily defeat us.

Some think they are prepared when they are not. This is typical of immature people. Children often take on more than they can handle. Because none of us likes to take the time necessary for preparation, it is very common to see people jump into things before they are ready. Preparation takes time. Immature people don't like to spend that necessary time.

Prepare thy work without, and make it fit for thyself in the field; and afterwards build thine house.
Proverbs 24:27

Now the end of the commandment is charity out of a pure heart, and of a good conscience, and of faith unfeigned: from which some having swerved have turned aside unto vain jangling; desiring to be teachers of the law; understanding neither what they say, nor whereof they affirm.

I Timothy 1:5-7

The word *swerved* means *to miss the mark, err, deviate from truth*. It is possible to mean well and still miss the mark. Truth with a little error mixed in is still not complete truth, and can be very dangerous. God has both a specific purpose for every life and a specific timetable for bringing forth that purpose. Many try to rush into something, only to discover that it wasn't the right place for them or, perhaps, the right time.

Another of the devices that satan uses is disorder, a distraction of focus. Because the call of God is to unity, the call of satan is to disunity and individualism. All ministries, ministers, and workers need to be under the covering provided when they are submitted to their set-man and to their church. Submission is a willing commitment and a joining, not a state of being dominated and overpowered. God joins you both to a man of God and to a local body of believers, making you part of the calling He has given the house. God owns you, and He wants you to work for a purpose, not for fifty-seven different purposes.

The Lord operates in families.

God setteth the solitary in families: He bringeth out those which are bound with chains: but the rebellious dwell in a dry land.

Psalm 68:6

Each of the individual ministries and ministers in a given church setting must focus on the general commission that God has given the set-man, thus using what they are specifically called to do to enhance that central vision of the house.

As we have seen, Paul urged the Corinthians:

...that ye all speak the same thing, and that there be no divisions among you; but that ye be perfectly joined together in the same mind and in the same judgment.

I Corinthians 1:10

The word *speak* here means *to lay forth, shew, describe or utter*. Speaking the same thing, having a common vision and a common goal can prevent *divisions*. The word for *divisions* here is *schisma*, meaning *a split or gap, a rent, a schism*. If we all have a common vision and speak the same things, we can prevent splits and schisms resulting from differences in opinion or doctrine.

God intends His Church *to be perfectly joined together*. The word is *katartizo* and means *to complete thoroughly, to repair, adjust or mend, fit and frame, prepare and restore*. The root words are *kata: distribution and intensity*, and *artios: fresh, complete, and perfect*.

God knows how to distribute people in positions to which they are fitted and framed. He knows how to restore and adjust His servants. He knows how to give us the same mind and understanding, and the same judgment, or purpose and will, so that there will be no schisms, quarrels, or strife. What a great God we serve!

Satan is adept at using our personal preferences for personalities as a tool for causing division. In God's scheme of things, however, the individual does not choose the apostle, set-man, or pastor to whom he or she submits. Only God can make that choice. The Corinthians had not yet learned that lesson when Paul wrote to them.

> *Now this I say, that every one of you saith, I am of Paul; and I of Apollos; and I of Cephas; and I of Christ. Is Christ divided? was Paul crucified for you? or were ye baptized in the name of Paul?*
>
> I Corinthians 1:12-13

Our adherence is not to a personality, but to God and to the man God chooses to place over you, for your own good. God knows what is best for you. We must trust Him. The Church begins like little children who want many of the wrong things. Fortunately, children have parents who know better how to make wise decisions. God wants to do the same for us spiritually. The person who can best serve as porter of your soul may not be the person you think can do it best. Trust God. He knows what He is doing.

Another of the tools satan has mastered is confusion.

> *For thus saith the Lord, That after seventy years be accomplished at Babylon I will visit you, and perform My good word toward you, in causing you to return to this place. For I know the thoughts that I think toward you, saith the Lord, thoughts of peace, and not of evil, to give you an expected end.*
>
> Jeremiah 29:10-11

Babylon means *confusion*. God has a precise plan for each one of us. We have a great destiny. Satan knows this and is determined to sidetrack us and stop us—any way that he can.

God has not destined us to Babylon. We are not destined to confusion. We are destined to greatness in God. Confusion can rob us of God's best. We need deliverance from Babylon, from confusion. When God brings us out of confusion, we are well on our way to His destined greatness. Therefore, satan will do everything he can to keep us in a state of confusion.

Many people are confused by their own dreams and desires. Often these desires are carnal and come to us from outside influences, from friends and family, from television, books or magazines, and not from God. Satan even has his own prophets.

For thus saith the Lord of hosts, the God of Israel; Let not your prophets and your diviners, that be in the midst of you, deceive you, neither hearken to your dreams which ye cause to be dreamed. For they prophesy falsely unto you in My name: I have not sent them, saith the Lord.
Jeremiah 29:8-9

Porters can do much to help the Church avoid the outside influence that causes confusion in our lives. A God-assigned set-man and a stable sheepfold will go far to protect you. A state of wandering from place to place can only put you in danger of attack. Moses knew what he was doing when he asked God to give His people a set-man.

Some people are particularly susceptible to deception, even Christians. Some of those who are most easily deceived by satan are those who are still drinking the *old wine* (see Luke 5:37-39). By *old wine* I mean prior moves of God or what God did in another period. Many are waiting for God to repeat something He did in the past, while He wants us to open up to the new things He has for us today. Stubbornly clinging to the old and refusing the new will drag you back, while God is trying to move you forward.

Jesus said:

Neither do men put new wine into old bottles: else the bottles break, and the wine runneth out, and the bottles perish: but they put new wine into new bottles, and both are preserved.

Matthew 9:17

New wine requires new bottles. Putting new into the old container doesn't work. The two are incompatible. Those who insist on the old wine are just hanging onto traditions which may now be meaningless.

While the Israelites were crossing the wilderness *en route* to the Promised Land, God told them to make a brass serpent so that they could be delivered from the snakes that had bitten and killed many. That metal snake served its purpose in the desert. God healed those who looked upon it with faith.

And Moses made a serpent of brass, and put it upon a pole, and it came to pass, that if a serpent had bitten any man, when he beheld the serpent of brass, he lived.

Numbers 21:9

The sad thing is: for the next nine hundred years the descendants of those people kept that now-useless brazen snake with them through their journeys. Hezekiah found it in the Temple, set up as an idol to which the Israelites burned incense.

He removed the high places, and brake the images, and cut down the groves, and brake in pieces the brasen serpent

that Moses had made: for unto those days the children of Israel did burn incense to it: and he called it Nehushtan.
II Kings 18:4

Nehushtan meant *a worthless hunk of tin.* Worthless things should be discarded. When the old was finally destroyed, Israel could get on with the new things God wanted to do for them.

It is very easy to keep looking to the past and to miss entirely the new things God is doing. The past was glorious. But we are not living in the past. God is the God of NOW. The present may be different from the past, but it is intended to be just as glorious, and even more so.

The Pharisees often talked with Jesus. They were so entrenched in tradition, however, that they could not really hear what He was saying.

Then came together unto Him the Pharisees, and certain of the scribes, which came from Jerusalem. And when they saw some of His disciples eat bread with defiled, that is to say, with unwashen, hands, they found fault. For the Pharisees, and all the Jews, except they wash their hands oft, eat not, holding the tradition of the elders. And when they come from the market, except they wash, they eat not. And many other things there be, which they have received to hold, as the washing of cups, and pots, brasen vessels, and of tables.

Then the Pharisees and scribes asked Him, Why walk not thy disciples according to the tradition of the elders, but eat bread with unwashen hands? He answered and said unto them, Well hath Esaias prophesied of you hypocrites, as it is written, This people honoureth Me with their lips, but their heart is far from Me. Howbeit in vain do they worship Me, teaching for doctrines the commandments of men. For laying aside the commandment of God, ye hold the tradition of men, as the washing of pots and cups: and many other such like things ye do.

And He said unto them, Full well ye reject the commandment of God, that ye may keep your own tradition. For Moses said, Honour thy father and thy mother; and, Whoso curseth father or mother, let him die the death: but ye say, If a man shall say to his father or mother, It is Corban, that is to say, a gift, by whatsoever thou mightest be profited by me; he shall be free. And ye suffer him no more to do ought for his father or his mother; making the word of God of none effect through your tradition, which ye have delivered: and many such like things do ye.

Mark 7:1-13

It is possible to *make the Word of God of none effect* through our tradition. Adherence to useless tradition makes us like those of whom Jeremiah prophesied:

Moab hath been at ease from his youth, and he hath settled on his lees, and hath not been emptied from vessel to vessel, neither hath he gone into captivity: therefore his taste remained in him, and his scent is not changed. Therefore, behold, the days come, saith the Lord, that I will send unto him wanderers, that shall cause him to wander, and shall empty his vessels, and break their bottles.

Jeremiah 48:11-12

God is sending wanderers to rid us of the old dregs and cause us to cry out for the new wine He has prepared. The word *wanderers* means *tilters*. It means "to tip over (for the purpose of spilling or pouring out), i.e. depopulate, to imprison or conquer." Men of God are tilters who take God's Word and tilt you over to pour out old wine. Then they use God's Word to break our bottles.

The Word of God cuts us apart to remove the bad and then restores us to something new and wonderful. It is a breaking process that empties us, like a pouring out of the old wine, so that God can give us a new bottle and fill it with the new. He is prepared to begin that process—if and when we are ready to submit to *the porter principle.*

Chapter 4

Adam, Porter of the Garden

And the Lord God planted a garden eastward in Eden; and there He put the man whom He had formed.
                                                            Genesis 2:8

God made Adam the first human porter. His primary area of responsibility was over the Garden of Eden. The word translated *planted* means *to fasten or strike in, like a stake hammered firmly into the ground*. The word *garden* refers to *a fenced garden* and is from the word *ganan*, which means *to hedge about, to protect and defend*. Clearly, Adam was to do more than tend vegetation in this plot of ground. He was to keep the place, to defend it. He was the first human porter.

The word translated *eastward* indicates *the front of a place*. It is from the Hebrew word for *precede, anticipate, hasten and prevent*. Adam was to meet or confront, oppose, and disappoint anything or anyone who would come against the garden, its contents, or its inhabitants. The garden was to be a protected place; and Adam was charged with protecting it.

Eden means *pleasure, delicate, delight, soft or pleasant.* Eden was originally intended to be a place of voluptuous living, a house of pleasure, producing, and delight for Adam and for all his descendants.

The Hebrew word for *placed* means far more than most people would read into that simple word. It means *appointed, ordained, and charged with certain duties.* These duties were twofold:

And the Lord God took the man, and put him into the garden of Eden to dress it and to keep it.

Genesis 2:15

The first duty of Adam was to dress the garden, or to work it. This included *tilling, serving, laboring as a husbandman, servant, and bondsman.* It also implied *to be enslaved and set a work, be a worshiper.* Adam was impressed into sacred duty.

Here the word *put* means *to deposit.* God specifically seized and accepted Adam to set him in the garden. Adam was the set-man of the Garden of Eden. God wanted Adam to be His first five-fold minister in all five facets, which are governing, guiding, grounding, guarding, and gathering or replenishing, but Adam didn't reach that maturity.

Adam's second duty was *to keep* the garden, be its porter. Adam was *to hedge it about, guard, protect, and attend to* it. The Hebrew also means *to beware, take heed to self, and look narrowly or observe, save and preserve.* This was a full-time commission given to Adam, and a vital one. He would have to be on the lookout for trouble. He was to be the watchman over the garden to judge whether to open or close the door to whoever wanted to come in. In this way, the garden would be kept safe and preserved.

Adam failed in his commission. Through his lack of proper porterage, the serpent was able to beguile him and to gain entrance. Satan bypassed Adam and went directly to the woman, bypassing God's order.

The Father is the head of Jesus. Jesus is the Head of the man. The man is the head of his wife and household. This was clearly outlined by the apostle Paul in writing to the Corinthians.

But I would have you know, that the head of every man is Christ; and the head of the woman is the man; and the head of Christ is God.

I Corinthians 11:3

Since every level of headship must earn respect, not demand it by force, more responsibility rests on the man to earn the respect of his woman than on the woman to submit to the headship of her man. You are not biblically the head until you qualify. Of course a man has to marry a woman who is marriage material for this principle to work. Not every man or every woman is marriage material. Due to past lack of training, discipline and example, there is much independence and over-bearing traits that reside in many. No one should get married if there is not proper understanding of marriage beforehand.

What is the husband's responsibility as head?

For the husband is the head of the wife, even as Christ is the head of the church: and He is the saviour of the body.

Ephesians 5:23

What a powerful word! The husband plays a vital part in becoming the savior of his wife's being. A proper husband is somewhat of an under-shepherd of his home under his set-man and leadership. The Hebrew for *head* is *kephale, the part most readily taken hold of, in the sense of seizing*. The man, then, places himself in satan's way, becoming a hedge of protection to his family. He is *the part most readily taken hold of*, which means strength, standing between the world and his wife, providing her the protection in their home as she needs. He is responsible for his wife's legitimate physical needs. He must keep her from harm and wrong. He must save and protect her. What a great responsibility!

In order to fulfill his God-given role, the man must be walking in more spiritual knowledge and wisdom than his wife. He must offer her strength and guidance, wisdom and knowledge. He must, in this way, earn her trust and respect. This means the man will have to spend more time with God and listening attentively to his set-man as he helps perfect his life.

> *Likewise, ye husbands, dwell with them according to knowledge, giving honour unto the wife, as unto the weaker vessel, and as being heirs together of the grace of life; that your prayers be not hindered.*
>
> I Peter 3:7

The wife is *the weaker vessel*. That means that she is more delicately made, more easily wounded, and more vulnerable—in some ways. The husband should be her source of strength, love, and understanding. His source of strength, in turn, is the Word of God. It is God, ultimately, who is in complete control of everyone concerned. This will not take place if you are not set in a church with a proper set-man with relevant Word of God coming forth. As churches grow in revelation, maturity, people and as the need arises, God brings forth mature leadership to help his set-man.

Both the husband and the wife have their divine responsibilities. The man, who is submitted to God, is to be the protector and provider for his wife. She, in turn, is to submit to his authority. This is not unreasonable, unspiritual, or unbiblical.

God's order has a purpose. It is not an imposition on us, but a blessing to us. The Lord never does anything that will result in our harm. He loves us more than we can know. Submitting to a loving and wise husband is not something to dread.

Submit does not mean being crushed underfoot; it means *to be in obedience, to submit self to, to subordinate.* Paul describes this submission as being *fit in the Lord.*

Wives, submit yourselves unto your own husbands, as it is fit in the Lord.

Colossians 3:18

Fit means *proper or right.* This is God's plan.

This does not make the wife less than her husband. She is his other part. She makes him complete. She is to bring forth the best in him just as good sheep are to bring forth the best in their set-man.

God has shown us the order of how this is to be accomplished.

Wives, submit yourselves unto your own husbands, as unto the Lord. For the husband is the head of the wife, even as

> *Christ is the head of the church: and He is the saviour of the body. Therefore as the church is subject unto Christ, so let the wives be to their own husbands in every thing. Husbands, love your wives, even as Christ also loved the church, and gave Himself for it; that He might sanctify and cleanse it with the washing of water by the word, that He might present it to Himself a glorious church, not having spot, or wrinkle, or any such thing; but that it should be holy and without blemish. So ought men to love their wives as their own bodies. He that loveth his wife loveth himself.*
> Ephesians 5:22-28

This love a husband is to have for his wife is expressed in the Greek word *agapao*. It is the kind of aggressive, seeking, and selfless love God has for us. A woman's love for her husband is expressed somewhat differently.

> *That they may teach the young women to be sober, to love their husbands, to love their children,*
>
> Titus 2:4

The word for *love* here is *philandros*. It means *fond of a man, affectionate as a wife*. If the husband will love his wife the way God loves her, the woman should love back with affection for him. This is called responsive love, just as the Church responds back to Christ as He loves them with agape love. Of course, just as Christ must have a Church that respects and can receive this kind of love, so must a husband have a wife as such. If husbands love their wives, they will do for their wives what Christ does for the Church. This is their responsibility in the Word. For example, as the porter of his house, the husband is responsible to intercede for his wife, as Christ does for the Church.

> *Wherefore He is able also to save them to the uttermost that come unto God by Him, seeing He ever liveth to make intercession for them.*
>
> Hebrews 7:25

A wife in return should respond back with intercession for her husband for him to remain stedfast in his God-given role.

Husbands are to love their wives *as their own bodies*. We take care of our bodies. We feed them and bathe them and otherwise care for them until they come to maturity. When they are sick, we nurse them to health.

Marriage is not just an initial physical joining. It is a spiritual lifelong commitment to cherish and care for the woman we love. As the man of his house, a husband becomes friend and lover to his wife. He takes on many of the duties once performed by her father. A wife is then to take on the trait of one being cared for, led and protected with proper response. When a man faithfully does this, it makes it easy for his wife to *reverence* him.

> *Nevertheless let every one of you in particular so love his wife even as himself; and the wife see that she reverence her husband.*
>
> Ephesians 5:33

The word used for *reverence* is *phobio, to be alarmed, revere, be in awe*. If the man becomes a fathering strength to a reasonable wife, she should not find it difficult to hold him in this kind of reverence. Proper informed women sense their true role in life, know innately that they were created for man, to be his help meet, who actually become the helper of his own species.

> *And the Lord God said, It is not good that the man should be alone; I will make him an help meet for him.*
>
> Genesis 2:18

God gave Adam a wife to be his right hand or again, the helper of his own species. He, in turn, was her porter, her spiritual head, providing her safety and covering. God placed Adam in the garden to be the porter, the bishop, the watchman, the overseer.

The serpent, in his cunning, did not go through the door and the doorkeeper, but *climbed up some other way*. He went directly to the woman, in circumvention of God's declared order.

> *Now the serpent was more subtil than any beast of the field which the Lord God had made. And he said unto the woman, Yea, hath God said, Ye shall not eat of every tree of the garden?*
>
> Genesis 3:1

The serpent came to the garden with a specific purpose. As the thief, he longs to steal, kill and destroy. The peace and harmony of the garden was an affront to him. He determined to destroy it. Being *more subtle than any beast of the field*, he knew how to do that.

He did not even attempt to go through Adam. He bypassed the authority of the garden and went directly to the woman. The wolf never goes through the shepherd. He goes directly to the sheep. As the apostle Paul said to the Ephesian pastors:

For I know this, that after my departing shall grievous wolves enter in among you, not sparing the flock.
Acts 20:29

The mistake of the woman was to enter into an agreement with the serpent without checking with her husband. Not only did she have a serious dialogue with him, she accepted what he was offering. She was totally out of order. She also misquoted what God had told Adam:

And the woman said unto the serpent, We may eat of the fruit of the trees of the garden: but of the fruit of the tree which is in the midst of the garden, God hath said, Ye shall not eat of it, neither shall ye touch it, lest ye die.
Genesis 3:2-3

God didn't say anything about touching the fruit. He said not to eat it. That's all. It was Adam's responsibility to see that his wife understood well what was expected of them, what they were free to do, and what they should avoid like the plague. When a person does not know what is expected of them, they become an easy prey to deception. It is our duty to make sure that each member of the family is well-informed.

We should not be surprised that satan refused to respect authority. He is a rebel. He always tries to bypass the shepherd and devastate the flock. While the children of Israel were crossing the wilderness, on their way to the Promised Land, satan began a dialogue with a man named Korah. Deceived by the enemy, Korah gathered a group of other respected men and tried to challenge the leadership of Moses

(Numbers 16:1-10). After all, he thought, they were just as holy, called and as anointed as Moses. But God did not take lightly their rebellion. The consequences they suffered were severe.

> *And it came to pass, as he had made an end of speaking all these words, that the ground clave asunder that was under them: and the earth opened her mouth, and swallowed them up, and their houses, and all the men that appertained unto Korah, and all their goods.*
>
> Numbers 16:31-32

God does not take lightly the actions of rebels. He is a God of order, and He expects us to follow His order—or else. Because Eve did not submit to the authority of her husband, this began a process whereby Eden was lost.

Adam was not guiltless in the matter. He had failed to earn Eve's respect. He failed in his responsibility as gatekeeper and allowed evil into the garden.

The results of neglecting or circumventing authority today are just as severe as they were in the time of Adam or in the time of Moses. Our refusal to set our house in order is one of the elements that is holding back the floodgates of revival, restoration and order upon the world today. God is ready—when we get ourselves ready.

Eve had no right to commit herself to a plan of action without first having spoken with her head. She should have gone back to her husband, who was set to be her protection, guidance, and salvation. She was not the head. She was the support system, the help meet of the man.

As the man is the image and glory of God, the woman is the glory of the man. God did not intend for the man to dominate his wife, but to lead, nurture and protect her. The two must be in constant communication. Nothing must be done independently of each other. This is a sacred partnership. The two should both know at all times where they are headed, what their general calling is, and what they need to accomplish that calling.

Adam made the same mistake as Eve. When he was confronted with the forbidden fruit, he did not check with his Head either. If he had, the fall could have been prevented. Conversations between husband and wife are not enough. If God is not given His proper place in our marriage, we are headed for disaster.

Adam rebelled too. He knew what God had told him, but he wanted to please his mate more than his Creator. He spoke and acted independently of his Head. He willingly left the safety and freedom of his covering. Such an act can only lead to tragedy.

What should Adam have done in this situation?

First, Adam should have been living more closely to the Lord so that he could better sense approaching danger. How did Eve get out of his sight and into a private place where the serpent could corner her and work his deception on her? Adam must have been lax in his duty as watchman. He should have sensed the presence of evil and driven satan from the garden and from his marriage. Again, the woman must manifest total cooperation with her God-given husband.

Secondly, Adam should have made sure that Eve understood perfectly the words of the Lord, what privileges they had, and why, and what was denied to them, and why. The command had been given to him. He needed to make sure that his wife understood it.

And the Lord God commanded the man, saying, Of every tree of the garden thou mayest freely eat: but of the tree of the knowledge of good and evil, thou shalt not eat of it: for in the day that thou eatest thereof thou shalt surely die.

Genesis 2:16-17

If Eve had understood the consequences of her actions, would she have eaten the forbidden fruit anyway? Probably not. If she had understood what DEATH meant, would she have insisted on disobeying? Probably not. DEATH should have been made more real to her.

When it became clear to Adam what his wife had done, he should have taken the responsibility for her failure. He should have repented immediately and asked her forgiveness. A reasonable wife would come under the submission of this. He should have refused to partake with her. He should have asked God exactly what to do in that sensitive situation. By his failure, Adam left the door open to the enemy.

It is easy to see why we have such a problem in America today. America is in rebellion against authority, and God moves through authority. America has grown to dislike and distrust order, and God is a God of order.

Disdaining the traditional (Christian) structure of the family, women have insisted on becoming dominant in the family. Disdaining the traditional (Christian) structure of the family, men have shirked their responsibility and become passive in the family. As a result, women cannot be blessed because they are not covered, and men cannot be blessed because they are not being responsible husbands and fathers.

We urgently need a revival and restoration of authority and order in the Body of Christ. Where are the porters?

Since men are expected to maintain order, the responsibility is ultimately ours. God ordained us to rule our households, not according to our own dictates and soulish or self control, not as dictators, not unjustly, but according to the Word of God and being accountable directly to Him. What are we waiting for? We must begin to put things in order if we expect our wives and children to be blessed of God.

The family unit is triune or a three-state structure, as is the individual: spirit, soul, and body. The man represents the spirit, which has the authority to rule. The woman represents soul, which should be in obedience and cooperation, as a willing aide to the spirit. The children represent the body, a manifestation or expression of the state and relationship between the spirit and soul.

Since the spirit is from God, the man can maintain his authority only as long as he is in God and of God. He has no authority of his own, apart from God. *The porter principle* requires that the man first learn to keep himself.

> *We know that whosoever is born of God sinneth not; but he that is begotten of God keepeth himself, and that wicked one toucheth him not.*
>
> I John 5:18

The man must be properly submitted to God and to the set-man and leaders of his sheepfold. He must recognize the importance of the five-fold ministry and be willing to submit to it, for his own edification and perfection. As head of the family, he must be regularly nurtured and grow. Only then can he think about keeping his household.

Some women are deceived by satan because they have no strong and stable husband who can stand in the vision of God and provide guidance. Men are notorious for leaving the spiritual responsibilities to their women. Paul warns that men who have a form of godliness but deny the power thereof can leave their wives uncovered, thus allowing others who are inspiried by satan to sway their women and lead them astray.

> *Having a form of godliness, but denying the power thereof: from such turn away. For of this sort are they which creep into houses, and lead captive silly women laden with sins, led away with divers lusts, ever learning, and never able to come to the knowledge of the truth.*
>
> II Timothy 3:5-7

The word here used for *silly, gunaikarion*, literally means *little or lean*. These people are lean in the Word of God, which would otherwise give them grounding—even if their heads, the husbands, are weak or ineffective. This is why it is important for the wife to consistently be in her church under her set-man so she can be matured and protected even if her husband is not responsible enough.

Women are very sensitive and can open up to God very easily. This makes them vulnerable, at times, to satanic deception. It was the woman who was first enticed by the serpent. He thought that if she could be convinced, she may convince her husband. This is the reason put forth by the apostle Paul for his often misused precaution to Timothy.

> *Let the woman learn in silence with all subjection. But I suffer not a woman to teach, nor to usurp authority over the man, but to be in silence. For Adam was first formed, then Eve. And Adam was not deceived, but the woman being deceived was in the transgression.*
>
> I Timothy 2:11-14

The apostle Paul did not intend this passage to convey the meaning that women cannot speak or do anything else in church. It only shows the proper order of her ministry (of teaching, prophesying, preaching and praying) under the authority of the men God has placed over her. God's system of order is for our protection, our shielding, and our covering and not for our harm.

Why should we, then, resist the order placed by a loving heavenly Father? Willingly submit yourself today to the order inherent in *the porter principle*.

Chapter 5

The Importance of a Church Home

Those that be planted in the house of the Lord shall flourish in the courts of our God.

Psalm 92:13

God, in His infinite wisdom, has placed porters—apostles, prophets, teachers, pastors and evangelists—in the Body of Christ to guard us from evil. Just as He placed porters around the throne of Heaven, God has placed porters in key positions in His Kingdom on earth. Just as the man is assigned the role of porter of the marriage and of the family, God places set-men to do the task of caring for and watching over the larger flock.

Sheep are very vulnerable to predators and need protection. Sheep easily stray and need to be kept in line. Sheep are slow to find green pastures and still waters and must be led to them.

Our loving heavenly Father strategically places His servants among the Church to work maturity in the Church. He sends the wanderers or tilters to divide us asunder and cut out the soulish flaws (Jeremiah 48:11-12). He sends those who will rid the Church of old wine and cause us to taste the new. He sends porters to guard and keep the gates. He knows how to protect and how to perfect His saints.

These men are so important. What they let in will get in, and what they keep out will be kept out.

And I will give unto thee the keys of the kingdom of heaven: and whatsoever thou shalt bind on earth shall be bound in heaven: and whatsoever thou shalt loose on earth shall be loosed in heaven.

Matthew 16:19

God entrusts this vital role to men. For these God-ordained men to be able to perform their assigned tasks, each Christian must be set in a church home, set within a spiritual family.

But now hath God set the members every one of them in the body, as it hath pleased Him.

I Corinthians 12:18

We are not given the privilege of choosing our place in the Body of Christ. God Himself reserves that right of choice. He knows what He is doing; He knows where we will flourish; He knows where we will grow best. He knows where He can best utilize our particular calling and talents. Why wrestle against His choice? Trust Him.

The responsibilities of those who are over us in the Lord are great. Their first duty is that of guardian or watchman.

Take ye heed, watch and pray: for ye know not when the time is. For the Son of man is as a man taking a far journey, who left his house, and gave authority to his servants, and to every man his work, and commanded the porter to watch. Watch ye therefore: for ye know not when the master of the house cometh, at even, or at midnight, or at the cockcrowing, or in the morning: lest coming suddenly he find you sleeping. And what I say unto you I say unto all, Watch.
Mark 13:33-37

Porters must be perceptive people. They cannot be asleep. They must *take heed*. They must *watch and pray*. They must be ever vigilant. The state of men's souls are at stake. The Son of Man has *commanded the porter to watch*. He is a warden at the gate.

Porters prepare the way for the coming of King Jesus.

Thy watchmen shall lift up the voice; with the voice together shall they sing: for they shall see eye to eye, when the Lord shall bring again Zion.
Isaiah 52:8

Accepting *the porter principle* and putting into operation the porter ministry will prepare the Church for the coming move of God. Seeing eye to eye means that God can only restore His Church back to their called place as they perceive and submit to God's commission that He gives and passes through His set-man of the flock.

There are many parallels: Just as the individual must willingly submit to the porter for this ministry to be effective, our coming King will not force Himself upon us. God works by His Spirit with those who are willing. When He finds people who are unwilling, He moves on and finds a remnant of those who are willing and gives His Kingdom to them instead.

Opening our hearts to the will of God allows Him to manifest all that He desires to do in us. Closing Him out causes the church to dry up and falter—because the Spirit of God is no longer at work there. Being grieved, He withdraws and seeks a welcome elsewhere.

Through the Reformation, God restored simple salvation back to the earth. Not everyone received it. Some churches continue as they were before the Reformation.

Through the Pentecostal movement God has restored the power of the Holy Ghost to the Church. Many have not received it, however, and go on as they were before this great outpouring began.

Teaching and the prophetic ministries have been restored to the Church. But not everyone has received them.

Finally, in these last days, God will restore apostolic order to anyone willing to hear and obey. Not everyone will receive it. Not every church is hearing the voice of God. Not every church has willing and eager members. Jesus said to the church at Laodicea:

Behold, I stand at the door, and knock: if any man hear My voice, and open the door, I will come in to him, and will sup with him, and he with Me.

Revelation 3:20

He was standing at the door, waiting to see if the Church was willing to open and let Him in. Now Jesus is standing at our door, knocking, and waiting to see if we will hear His voice and let Him in. Our door is the *psuche* or the soul. The soul is the part of you that the porter has the oversight of so God can build your spirit man into more perfection.

The word used here for *voice* means *an address for any purpose*. Christ discloses His presence, but does not yell out or force Himself upon us. If we open the door which is our soul (mind, emotions, will, or our self life), He will come in and dine with us. Satan, to the contrary, is anything but a gentleman. He walks around like a roaring lion, seeking those whom he can devour (see First Peter 5:8).

Jesus is seeking entrance to the door of your heart which is the soul. Let Him in. Satan is seeking entrance to the door of your heart. He must be kept out—at any cost.

We desperately need a restoration of the porter ministry in the Church today. By looking at the Old Testament pattern, we can get an idea of what God wants to do in the Church today.

> *And the porters were, Shallum, and Akkub, and Talmon, and Ahiman, and their brethren: Shallum was the chief;*
>   I Chronicles 9:17

A chief porter was appointed. In this case, his name was Shallum. *Shallum* means *recompense for a benefit or for an injury, to make at peace or make good, finish, and restore.* Shallum was a porter of peace, bringing peace in spirit, mind, and body. He was serving God's primary or chief purpose, that of bringing and keeping peace.

Akkub was the porter of restraint and ambush, the porter of protection. His name means *to lie in wait, to smell out as sitting on a web, to seize by the heel, to restrain.* The Akkubs which God place in the Church protect us from intruders, by force, if necessary. They will "trip up" any intruder who tries to get past them. The name Akkub also implies one that is more dangerous than he may at first appear. God has His Akkubs standing guard.

Talmon was the porter who would suddenly leap on, oppress and frighten any intruder. His name is the same as the word for a leaping insect. *Talmon* means *oppressive and to be dismayed*. The Talmons whom God appoints over the Church will leap suddenly to attack an approaching enemy. They jump on him before he knows what has happened.

Ahiman is the porter who lets in what God has for you and keeps out what satan tries to slip by the gate. His name means *brother of a portion, or gift, a part of, whether and neither*. It also means *to apportion; apart; hence a musical chord* (as parted into strings); *defective*. So Ahiman is able to hear discord like no one else. Ministrels who are in harmony with God and the set-man are able to make sweet incense. Minstrels who are not in harmony with God and the set-man make sounds of discord. Satan likes to control the gates of thanksgiving and the courts of praise. So, Ahiman helps porter the music ministry of the Church and the flow of unity in the house. Ahiman hates discord whether it be in music or in any sound from anyone's lips. When someone approaches the door, Ahiman decides whether they are allowed to come in or not. He decides whether or not we need what is being offered. If the thing will not be a gift to the people, (in other words, if it is not of the Lord), God's Ahimans won't allow it to enter.

Besides Shallum, Akkub, Talmon, and Ahiman, the Scriptures mention *"their brethren."* These *brethren* were porters of the same family, kindred, of like kind, of a similar purpose and ability.

The Importance of a Church Home 59

These four men—Shallum, Akkub, Talmon, and Ahiman—were given the responsibility of the east gate of the king's palace. The East is where the sun rises, where the day begins. The men set over the east gate were to provide an example for others to follow. The East is the beginning of all things. These porters of the east are to let in what God wants in and keep out anything God wants kept out.

Other men served as porters of the north, south and west. The king was guarded on every side.

Shallum was descended from a very important and powerful man. His name was *Kore*, which means *preach or proclaim, from the idea of accosting a man*. He and his family were found to be very responsible people and were given charge of the gates, the all-important limit or threshold to the city. This family was trusted to guard these entrances diligently and to preserve the integrity of the city.

Another famous porter was named Zechariah. He was the porter of the door of the tabernacle of the congregation. *Zechariah* means *Jah (Jehovah) has remembered*. Zechariah's father's name was *Meshelemiah*, which means *ally of Jah, or in agreement with God*. We need many Zechariahs and many Meshelemiahs today, men who are in agreement with God.

King David and Samuel, the seer, began the restoration of the ministry of porters. They examined each man who was to be considered for this all-important position. The name *David* means *boiling love*. It was David's great love for God and the people that led him to set their house in order. *Samuel* means *heard of God*. Because Samuel had an ear sensitive to hear the voice of God, his voice was also heard on high.

All these which were chosen to be porters in the gates were two hundred and twelve. These were reckoned by their

> *genealogy in their villages, whom David and Samuel the seer did ordain in their set office.*
>
> I Chronicles 9:22

The porters of David's day were *reckoned by their genealogy*, much like a purebred animal. Now porters of the house are appointed and set in office by God through His set-man.

These Old-Testament porters were ordained *in their set office*. These men were found to be totally trustworthy, faithful, and stable. They would not attempt to overthrow those over them, but would support them, standing solidly at their right hand. Because they had proven trustworthy, to them was given the oversight of the entrance and the house of God by posts or by wards.

> *So they and their children had the oversight of the gates of the house of the Lord, namely, the house of the tabernacle, by wards.*
>
> I Chronicles 9:23

The Tabernacle was a covering for the people, just as the Church of today should be. The porters were ordained to safeguard the integrity of the Tabernacle and were, therefore, over the safety of the people. Nothing was to remain unguarded.

> *In four quarters were the porters, toward the east, west, north, and south.*
>
> I Chronicles 9:24

The Hebrew words used here are interesting. The word translated *four* is from *raba*, which means *to sprawl at all fours, to be four-sided, and to square or lie out flat, especially in regard to copulation*. The word translated *quarters* is the same word for *spirit*. The *east*, again, is where the sun rises. *West* means *to roar like noisy surf* (the Mediterranean Sea was to the west of Israel). The sun sets in the west, denoting accomplishment or completion. *North* means *gloomy and unknown, hidden.* North refers to the undiscovered, secret things of God. *South* means *parched,* from the drought in that region.

Our spirits need to be in unity or conjunction with the Spirit of God in every aspect or direction of our lives. We need to be in spiritual intercourse with God at the beginning of every situation, as well as at the end; at sunrise and sunset; even when things are roaring or turbulent.

We need to be joined with God in the north, when hidden dark or gloom surrounds our situation and we don't know what to do, when we don't know what undisclosed things God has for us. As we seek God in His North dwelling place, He will reveal to us those hidden and undiscovered things for our life that only He knows. Living in the north is living in the secret revelational chamber of God. And we need to remain joined with God even when we are in the south, when we are parched. We must be seeking God, hearing His Word, praising and worshiping and opening ourselves to Him at all times and in every situation, so that He can manifest all that He has for our lives.

And their brethren, which were in their villages, were to come after seven days from time to time with them.
I Chronicles 9:25

Other porters were periodically needed. When men were found who had reached the necessary maturity, they could be used. They were to come *after seven days* and *from time to time.* Seven is the number of completeness. When God's work is complete in your life, you can stand with the porters.

From time to time it may be noticed that other brothers have risen to maturity, have become serious and dedicated and are ready to serve. God is searching for such brothers to be porters of His house. In the meantime, let us each submit to the assigned porters, knowing that they labor for our spiritual, mental, emotional, volitional and physical welfare.

God is faithful. When He assigns people to porter our souls, He gives them a godly love for us that causes them to feed us with God's relevant Word.

> *And I will give you pastors according to Mine heart, which shall feed you with knowledge and understanding.*
>
> Jeremiah 3:15

Recognizing that they are of God and are working for our good, we must join with them in spirit, as the Ephesians did with the apostle Paul (see Acts 20:36-37).

When God joins us to others for our mutual benefit, it is just as serious a joining as a marriage. And, in a marriage, we are instructed to be careful that no man separate us. This is called God-given relationships. Jesus talked about God-given relationships in John 17 as He said: "them which Thou hast given Me" (John 17:9).

Most of the New Testament teaching that we use as admonition to the marriage was actually given to the Church and is to be applied just as strictly to the Church relationship as it is to the marriage relationship.

> *Wives, submit yourselves unto your own husbands, as unto the Lord. For the husband is the head of the wife,* **even as Christ is the head of the church:** *and He is the saviour of the body. Therefore* **as the church is subject unto Christ,** *so let the wives be to their own husbands in every thing.*

Husbands, love your wives, **even as Christ also loved the church, and gave Himself for it; that He might sanctify and cleanse it with the washing of water by the word, that He might present it to Himself a glorious church, not having spot, or wrinkle, or any such thing; but that it should be holy and without blemish.** *So ought men to love their wives as their own bodies. He that loveth his wife loveth himself. For no man ever yet hated his own flesh; but nourisheth and cherisheth it,* **even as the Lord the church: for we are members of His body, of His flesh, and of His bones.** *For this cause shall a man leave his father and mother, and shall be joined unto his wife, and they two shall be one flesh. This is a great mystery: but* **I speak concerning Christ and the church.**

Ephesians 5:22-32

Marriage is an analogy of the Church. The way the Church is to work is the way a good marriage of husband and wife works. A good marriage in proper order is an earthly-spiritual expression of how God's Church is supposed to be. When God joins us together, we must not allow anything or anyone to separate us.

Wherefore they are no more twain, but one flesh. What therefore God hath joined together, let not man put asunder.

Matthew 19:6

The word *joined* means *union, to yoke together, with by process, possession, instrumentality, companionship, and resemblance; beside with completeness.* This is what God does for us when He joins us with His set-man and those of that sheepfold. If He thinks enough of us to do that, who are we to break these divinely-appointed relationships?

Satan is always trying to keep apart what God has destined to be joined together. And he is forever striving to force apart what God has already joined together. He is intent on stealing the commission or vision—as soon as it has been planted.

Jesus gave us the Parable of the Sower, in which He clearly showed satan, as *the fowls*, attempting to snatch away the good seed before it has time to take root.

And He spake many things unto them in parables, saying, Behold, a sower went forth to sow; and when he sowed, some seeds fell by the way side, and the fowls came and devoured them up: some fell upon stony places, where they had not much earth: and forthwith they sprung up, because they had no deepness of earth: and when the sun was up, they were scorched; and because they had no root, they withered away. And some fell among thorns; and the thorns sprung up, and choked them: but other fell into good ground, and brought forth fruit, some an hundredfold, some sixtyfold, some thirtyfold. Who hath ears to hear, let him hear.

Matthew 13:3-9

Someone must take authority over satan and his desires, bind him, and take back all that he has stolen. He is the strong man, whose house we must spoil. The only way this can be done is by bringing the soul (mind, emotions, will or our self life) into subjection to God's Word. Just binding the devil with your mouth will not do it. You must come under the authority of God in His Word. God's set-man or porter along with the proper leadership in your church takes the oversight of your soul through God's Word. So the *psuche* or soul must first be pulled in line by consistent Word and order from your set-man and assigned leadership. If just verbal binding would have accomplished this, many would be in proper order today. It requires the work of the porter. The set-man in himself has no right to bring anyone's soul in line by any means other than the Word and Spirit of God. When we obey God's Word and order, satan is bound and defeated.

Or else how can one enter into a strong man's house, and spoil his goods, except he first bind the strong man? and then he will spoil his house.
Matthew 12:29

Only when the strong man has been bound and defeated can God work out His purpose in our lives. Few have become fully aware of the seriousness of this divine joining. Relatively few understand the importance of the scriptural admonition.

Not forsaking the assembling of ourselves together, as the manner of some is; but exhorting one another: and so much the more, as ye see the day approaching.
Hebrews 10:25

When men learn to come under the porterage system of the House of God, they, in turn, will learn to guard their households. God's people will be in proper order from the largest Body of Christ to the smallest bishoprick (an individual). Then every aspect of our lives will be defended, watched over, and secured. What a marvelous plan God has designed!

Satan would love to displace every set-man whom God has ordained and placed. We must take a stand against his attempts to do so. Just as it is important for each of us to remain in place under our set-man, it is important for each set-man to hold his ground. The Church must not allow satan to run their man of God off. If Jesus set him in that place, he must stand his ground. Let satan and his people get out! Let God's set-man and God's people stay in their appointed place! This is a vital element of *the porter principle*.

Chapter 6

The Danger of Relinquishing Control to Satan

And Jesus said, For judgment I am come into this world, that they which see not might see; and that they which see might be made blind. And some of the Pharisees which were with Him heard these words, and said unto Him, Are we blind also? Jesus said unto them, If ye were blind, ye should have no sin: but now ye say, We see; therefore your sin remaineth.

John 9:39-41

Jesus said that He had come into the world for judgment, *that they which see not might see; and that they which see might be made blind.* He told the Pharisees that, because they said, *"We see,"* their sin remained. The problem of the Pharisees was that they were living in the past. Their tradition blinded them to the new things God was doing. Because they were sure they saw and understood everything, they were blind, Jesus said. If they had admitted that they could not see and understand everything, He was willing to give them new sight. God is a Revealer of secrets. He always leads His sheep into clarity—if they are willing to follow Him.

True sheep do not follow the voice of a stranger or an impostor. They recognize the voice of authority and love. If we are willing, God will lead us, using the under-shepherds and under-bishops He has set, and will enable us to recognize His voice through others. When you knowingly reject the will of God for your life, you become blinded and relinquish control of your life to satan.

When Adam failed to keep or guard properly everything that God had entrusted to him, he unwittingly surrendered control of his life, his family, and his future to satan. In a sense, satan became the porter of Adam's life. And, when satan is allowed to keep the door, to control the flow of activity, he knows how to keep God out.

Satan delights in being the bishop of your soul. He loves to rule over your mind, your emotions and your will. The apostle Paul revealed satan's methods to the Thessalonians.

> *Let no man deceive you by any means: for that day shall not come, except there come a falling away first, and that man of sin be revealed, the son of perdition; who opposeth and exalteth himself above all that is called God, or that is worshipped; so that he as God sitteth in the temple of God, shewing himself that he is God.*
>
> II Thessalonians 2:3-4

God's Word tells us that we are the temple of God. Even though God has corporate assemblages, we are also individual temples that God lives in. We are a part of God's corporate temple. If satan can control our thinking, he can control us. If he can control our power to reason, he can influence our every decision. In this way, he can also weaken our spirits and control our bodies. It is impossible to have a holy body, while, at the same time, having a weak spirit and an unholy mind. The mind controls the body. If satan is sitting on the throne of your mind, he is your god.

Since the fall of Adam and Eve came about through disorder, through bypassing the proper authority, we can see how very important God's order is in maintaining our spiritual lives. Operating independently of proper spiritual authority is suicidal. Why take the risk? Why hand satan authority on a silver platter?

Anything out of apostolic order is rebellion, and rebellion plays into the hands of the rebel, himself. Rebellion is not of God. Rebellion caused many of the Israelites to perish in the wilderness. When Joshua led the remaining children of Israel into the Promised Land, he knew they would prosper—only if rebellion was not found in them.

The Lord God of gods, the Lord God of gods, He knoweth, and Israel He shall know; if it be in rebellion, or if in transgression against the Lord, (save us not this day,)
Joshua 22:22

Saul, the first king of Israel, lost his position and, eventually, his life because of rebellion. When we leave out the words in italics that were added by the translators, we see the truth concerning rebellion and stubbornness:

For rebellion the sin of witchcraft, and stubbornness iniquity and idolatry. Because thou hast rejected the word of the Lord, He hath also rejected thee from being king.
I Samuel 15:23

So rebellion *is the sin of* witchcraft, and *stubbornness iniquity and idolatry* or stubbornness equals iniquity and idolatry.

Today, we are living in a rebellious world. Children are rebellious; wives are rebellious; students are rebellious; workers are rebellious; citizens are rebellious. As Christians, however, we cannot allow our inheritance to be snatched away because of rebellion. Rebellion is witchcraft and results in your relinquishing everything.

Rebellion and stubbornness resulted in Adam's being cast out of the garden that God had prepared especially for him and his family.

> *So He drove out the man; and He placed at the east of the garden of Eden Cherubims, and a flaming sword which turned every way, to keep the way of the tree of life.*
>
> **Genesis 3:24**

Adam lost eternal life; he lost his health; he lost the prosperity the garden provided; he lost his peace of mind; he lost everything. He relinquished control of his life to a thief who was intent on stealing and destroying. What a terrible price to pay!

Satan opposes everything that is of God. It is a terrible mistake to relinquish control of your life, knowingly or unknowingly, to such a one. When he gains control, he even deceives his subjects into thinking that he is God, that what he is doing is the best thing for them. He distorts their thinking and warps their souls. We must not give him the chance.

In many Christian circles, rebellion is thought of as a wholesome thing. Some Christians proudly label themselves as rebels. In some groups, each person is his own head, whether he/she qualifies for that position or not. Insubordination is thought of as a merit. What a twisted concept! These people are accidents waiting to happen. They are nothing but loose mules, wandering stars, and birds without a nest.

> *As a bird that wandereth from her nest, so is a man that wandereth from his place.*
>
> Proverbs 27:8

The word *wandereth* here means *to rove, flee, or depart.* A *nest*, on the other hand, is *a fixed dwelling.* This word *place* is *a standing, a condition of body or mind.* Both nest and place are representative of the church body to which the Lord has assigned you, under a set-man.

When rebellion reigns in Christian circles, the people *despise dominion and speak evil of dignities.*

> *Likewise also these filthy dreamers defile the flesh, despise dominion, and speak evil of dignities.*
>
> Jude 1:8

This letter was written to Christians, not to unbelievers. It is possible to be called *Christian* and still be in rebellion and under the influence of satan.

When you *despise* God's government, you *reject* and *neutralize* it, *disesteem* and *set* it *aside.* You can only do this under deception.

Satan's lie is that submission to God and to His leaders will rob you of the freedom and happiness you deserve. Nothing could be further from the truth! Leaders who are placed by God are accountable to Him. They are not tyrants with selfish aims and whims. Those who shrug them off, violate them, and cast them aside are self-willed and presumptuous, venturing into arrogance, and relinquishing control of their lives to the evil one.

The righteous angels are wise. They are in total subjection to God and to their overseers. Michael, in speaking to satan concerning the body of Moses, revealed his deep respect for God-given authority.

> *Yet Michael the archangel, when contending with the devil he disputed about the body of Moses, durst not bring against him a railing accusation, but said, The Lord rebuke thee.*
>
> Jude 9

Even though lucifer was long-since fallen, Michael left rebuke to God. A similar truth about the respect among angels is expressed in the apostle Peter's second letter to the churches.

> *But chiefly them that walk after the flesh in the lust of uncleanness, and despise government. Presumptuous are they, selfwilled, they are not afraid to speak evil of dignities. Whereas angels, which are greater in power and might, bring not railing accusation against them before the Lord.*
>
> II Peter 2:10-11

Jude calls these people *clouds without water, trees whose fruit withereth, raging waves of the sea, foaming out their own shame, and wandering stars, to whom is reserved the blackness of darkness for ever.* What powerful language!

> *These are spots in your feasts of charity, when they feast with you, feeding themselves without fear: clouds they are*

without water, carried about of winds; trees whose fruit withereth, without fruit, twice dead, plucked up by the roots; raging waves of the sea, foaming out their own shame; wandering stars, to whom is reserved the blackness of darkness for ever.

Jude 12-13

The apostle Peter calls these people *spots and blemishes, cursed children and wells without water.*

And shall receive the reward of unrighteousness, as they that count it pleasure to riot in the day time. Spots they are and blemishes, sporting themselves with their own deceivings while they feast with you; having eyes full of adultery, and that cannot cease from sin; beguiling unstable souls: an heart they have exercised with covetous practices; cursed children: which have forsaken the right way, and are gone astray, following the way of Balaam the son of Bosor, who loved the wages of unrighteousness; but was rebuked for his iniquity: the dumb ass speaking with man's voice forbad the madness of the prophet.

These are wells without water, clouds that are carried with a tempest; to whom the mist of darkness is reserved for ever. For when they speak great swelling words of vanity, they allure through the lusts of the flesh, through much wantonness, those that were clean escaped from them who live in error. While they promise them liberty, they themselves are the servants of corruption: for of whom a man is overcome, of the same is he brought in bondage. For if after they have escaped the pollutions of the world through the knowledge of the Lord and Saviour Jesus Christ, they are again entangled therein, and overcome, the latter end is worse with them than the beginning.

> II Peter 2:13-20

The prognosis is not good for those who reject God's authority over their lives.

Woe unto them! for they have gone in the way of Cain, and ran greedily after the error of Balaam for reward, and perished in the gainsaying of Core.

> Jude 11

They will, Peter said, *utterly perish in their own corruption.* They will *receive the reward of unrighteousness.* What a dreadful end! The need to respect godly authority is clear.

Some teachers have been guilty of spreading disorder. By teaching that every person has his/her own ministry, without teaching how the ministries relate to one another and submit to one another, they have thrust forth a whole army of independent ministers, who are accountable to no one, and who spread disorder wherever they go.

As witness to this fact, tens of thousands of new ministries have been registered with the government in recent years. Are these ministries building the Kingdom of God or building an independent kingdom?

It is true that every person in the Body of Christ has a ministry. Every person has some special gift. But none of the gifts or ministries operates independently. All are interrelated. Peter spoke of Judas:

For he was numbered with us, and had obtained part of this ministry.

> Acts 1:17

Judas had *part of this ministry*. He was not a loose canon. None of the apostles saw their work as something separate from the whole. Each of them was laboring for the benefit of the whole Body. Even though each of us are to come into relationship with only those that God gives us, we are still a part of the whole universal Church.

The term *wandering stars* used by Jude was one the ancients used for the planets. Because the planets constantly shifted their position in the night sky, they were thought of as *wandering stars*. This term came to mean something or somebody *having no fixed course or purpose, an erratic, random wanderer, transported some distance from its original source and roving like a tramp*. It was anything but a complimentary term!

There is nothing good about being a rebel. No good can come of leaving the place where God has set you in the family. No good can come of taking a stand against God, against the Word of God or against the set-man God has placed over you. Rebellion plays into satan's hands and gives him free reign in your life.

Make a decision. Who will sit on the throne of your life, controlling your mind, your emotions and your will? When women insist on playing the dominant role in the family and men insist on playing the passive role in the family, both are playing into the hands of the enemy.

Being strong and outgoing doesn't necessarily mean you are dominating. And being quiet doesn't necessarily mean you are passive. But get God's order and maintain it—for the benefit of everyone concerned.

It should be a frightening thought to every believer to realize that it is possible to be a Christian (and even to be baptized with the Spirit) and still receive satanic influence over your soul. The very thought should compel each of us to learn all there is to know about God's will for our lives and to willingly and joyfully submit to His will.

We hear Christians saying: "I love God, but I hate that guy." This shows us how satan can influence the mind, emotions and will of a believer. We blame many of our faults on heredity. He was *just born with a bad temper*, we think, or *she is just moody by nature*. We call it a character flaw. The truth is that satan is exercising lordship over the souls of many Christians, without them even being aware of what he is doing.

In a case like that of the madman of Gadara, it is easy for anyone to see the influence of satan on his being. Because he was totally indwelt by demons and possessed beyond any question, who could doubt it?

And they arrived at the country of the Gadarenes, which is over against Galilee. And when He went forth to land, there met Him out of the city a certain man, which had devils long time, and ware no clothes, neither abode in any house, but in the tombs. When he saw Jesus, he cried out, and fell down before Him, and with a loud voice said, What have I to do with thee, Jesus, Thou Son of God most high? I beseech Thee, torment me not. (For He had commanded the unclean spirit to come out of the man. For oftentimes it had caught him: and he was kept bound with chains and in fetters; and he brake the bands, and was driven of the devil into the wilderness.) And Jesus asked him, saying, What is thy name? And he said, Legion: because many devils were entered into him. And they besought Him that He would not command them to go out into the deep.

And there was there an herd of many swine feeding on the mountain: and they besought Him that He would suffer them to enter into them. And He suffered them. Then went the devils out of the man, and entered into the swine: and the herd ran violently down a steep place into the lake, and were choked.

Luke 8:26-33

Other cases of satan's influence are not so obvious: for instance, the subtle influence he exerted on the mind of Peter. When Jesus spoke to Peter of His impending death, Peter reacted badly.

Then Peter took Him, and began to rebuke Him, saying, Be it far from Thee, Lord: this shall not be unto Thee.

Matthew 16:22

The marginal notations in some Bibles concerning the original Greek of the phrase *this shall not be unto Thee* says: *Pity Thyself.* In other words, *think about Yourself and avoid this thing.* You don't have to do it. Jesus responded to Peter's suggestion with harsh words.

But He turned, and said unto Peter, Get thee behind Me, Satan: thou art an offence unto Me: for thou savourest not the things that be of God, but those that be of men.

Matthew 16:23

Peter was not demon possessed. He was a disciple of Jesus. But Jesus sensed that satan was influencing the thinking of Peter in this case. When He spoke, He did not address His words directly to Peter. He spoke to satan who had influenced Peter to think selfish thoughts. As Peter's set-man, Jesus took control of the situation and rebuked the enemy who was trying to mount the throne of Peter's soul.

Satan does not parade in horns and tail. He disguises himself. He often disguises himself as someone else's personality. He often disguises himself as a worthy religious thought. Just because we love God, pay our tithes, and speak in tongues and prophesy doesn't make us immune to the attacks of the evil one. To the contrary, the fact that we love God makes us a target for satan's devices.

When a person finds himself/herself under satanic influence, the first thing he/she must do is resist and repent and turn back to the Shepherd and Bishop of our souls, who is Jesus. Only He can free us, and only as we invite Him to take His rightful place as Lord of our lives.

Those who have rebelled, have rebelled against God. Those who have strayed, have strayed from His watchful eye. Because our rebellion is directed at Him, our repentance and return must be directed, first, to Him.

Secondly, making Jesus Lord involves submitting to the authorities God has placed over us for our benefit. If we have truly repented of our rebellion, we will willingly and joyfully submit to God's will. This act will restore His favor upon our lives and remove the possibility that satan might gain access to all that we own. By doing this, we effectively shut him out.

Why would we do anything else? *The porter principle* was designed by a loving God for our benefit. Thank Him for it. And don't run the risk of losing God's protection and blessing by rebelling against God's best for your life.

Chapter 7

Recognizing and Avoiding Dangerous Influences

Now we have received, not the spirit of the world, but the spirit which is of God; that we might know the things that are freely given to us of God.

I Corinthians 2:12

Other people, who don't always have the right spirit, can influence us for evil. It is very common for people to make up their minds based on what others around them are saying and thinking. Children often have all the same fears and prejudices their parents have. The members of a church often have all the same tendencies their pastor has.

Among young people, we call this influence *peer pressure*. It is a pressure to conform, to be like others, to think and act as those around us. Attitudes are contagious.

This truth is reflected in the tendency toward all types of fads. The fads that we most easily recognize are fads in dress and hair style. But fads are just as real in all other matters of life.

Following the lead of others, however, is much more than a question of influence or peer pressure. It is the work of a spirit. There is a spirit of the world which is contagious. It emanates, of course, from satan himself. Just as we can have the power to impart the Spirit of God to others, the spirit of the world can be imparted to those who are susceptible and open to it.

When the Spirit of God is moving, those whose hearts are open are affected. They feel God moving and respond. When the apostle Peter preached on the Day of Pentecost, the anointing upon him affected many of those who heard him, as well. They were convicted of their sins and drawn to God. They asked Peter what they could do to receive the blessing of God.

Now when they heard this, they were pricked in their heart, and said unto Peter and to the rest of the apostles, Men and brethren, what shall we do?

Acts 2:37

When the apostle Paul was preaching in Lystra, a lame man was captivated by the Spirit of God and responded:

And there they preached the gospel. And there sat a certain man at Lystra, impotent in his feet, being a cripple from his mother's womb, who never had walked: the same heard Paul speak: who stedfastly beholding him, and perceiving that he had faith to be healed, said with a loud voice, Stand upright on thy feet. And he leaped and walked.

Acts 14:7-10

The Holy Spirit is also conveyed by the laying on of hands. When Peter took by the hand the lame man he encountered at the gate Beautiful, the man was healed (see Acts 3:7).

When Peter and John laid hands on the Samaritans and prayed for them to receive the Holy Ghost, they did.

Now when the apostles which were at Jerusalem heard that Samaria had received the word of God, they sent unto them Peter and John: who, when they were come down, prayed for them, that they might receive the Holy Ghost: (for as yet He was fallen upon none of them: only they were baptized in the name of the Lord Jesus.) Then laid they their hands on them, and they received the Holy Ghost.

Acts 8:14-17

When Paul laid hands on some disciples of John for the same purpose, they spoke in tongues and prophesied.

And when Paul had laid his hands upon them, the Holy Ghost came on them; and they spake with tongues, and prophesied.

Acts 19:6

The spirit of satan, or an evil spirit, can also be imparted. For instance, a person can start talking about satan and the whole atmosphere changes.

If you listen too long to someone criticizing a man of God or a church, that spirit of criticism will soon begin to oppress you. Miriam adversely affected Aaron in this way (see Numbers 12:1-9), and Korah dragged down a whole group of Israelites (see Numbers 16:1-3). When someone begins to criticize those God has placed in positions of authority, those who listen are bound to be adversely affected.

Many are more readily influenced by wrong, in this regard, than they influence others for good. The Lord wants us to be more like television stations than like television sets. Let us be the transmitters, not the receivers. Instead of allowing the evil in people around us to influence us, we should change those around us with our good influence. Most people are followers; few are leaders.

When the spies returned from their foray into the Promised Land, most of the Israelites were more ready to listen to those with a bad report than to the two who had a good report. But God honored Joshua and Caleb for standing against the current of bad attitude and for believing what He had told them.

> *But My servant Caleb, because he had another spirit with him, and hath followed Me fully, him will I bring into the land whereinto he went; and his seed shall possess it.*
>
> Numbers 14:24

Joshua and Caleb were the only two of their generation who were allowed to cross over into the Promised Land when the time came. Everyone else perished on the other side of the Jordan.

Those who oppose God and His servants have a dangerous spirit. The danger is not to the mature, but to the children in faith. Immature believers are often moved by the wrong voices.

> *Also of your own selves shall men arise, speaking perverse things, to draw away disciples after them.*
>
> Acts 20:30

In every crowd, satan has his servants who are present only to cause trouble. These are the modern-day Korahs.

Recognizing and Avoiding Dangerous Influences 83

Now when they had passed through Amphipolis and Apollonia, they came to Thessalonica, where was a synagogue of the Jews: and Paul, as his manner was, went in unto them, and three sabbath days reasoned with them out of the scriptures, opening and alleging, that Christ must needs have suffered, and risen again from the dead; and that this Jesus, whom I preach unto you, is Christ. And some of them believed, and consorted with Paul and Silas; and of the devout Greeks a great multitude, and of the chief women not a few. But the Jews which believed not, moved with envy, took unto them certain lewd fellows of the baser sort, and gathered a company, and set all the city on an uproar, and assaulted the house of Jason, and sought to bring them out to the people. And when they found them not, they drew Jason and certain brethren unto the rulers of the city, crying, These that have turned the world upside down are come hither also; whom Jason hath received: and these all do contrary to the decrees of Caesar, saying that there is another king, one Jesus. And they troubled the people and the rulers of the city, when they heard these things. And when they had taken security of Jason, and of the other, they let them go. And the brethren immediately sent away Paul and Silas by night unto Berea:

Acts 17:1-10

These men were not satisfied that Paul had left their city. They felt compelled to follow him to the next city and to be sure that he was mistreated and driven out there too.

...who coming thither went into the synagogue of the Jews. These were more noble than those in Thessalonica, in that they received the word with all readiness of mind, and searched the scriptures daily, whether those things

were so. Therefore many of them believed; also of honourable women which were Greeks, and of men, not a few. But when the Jews of Thessalonica had knowledge that the word of God was preached of Paul at Berea, they came thither also, and stirred up the people. And then immediately the brethren sent away Paul to go as it were to the sea: but Silas and Timotheus abode there still.

Acts 17:10-14

God speaks boldly and clearly with regard to anything or anyone that comes against His Church, His commission, His man or His people. He warns against the venom of division inspired by satan. It can be deadly. When a venomous viper bites you, he infects you with the same venom that he has. When a venomus person bites you with their influence, the same is true also.

Follow peace with all men, and holiness, without which no man shall see the Lord: looking diligently lest any man fail of the grace of God; lest any root of bitterness springing up trouble you, and thereby many be defiled;

Hebrews 12:14-15

This word *defiled* means *contaminated* or we could say infected. Satan uses people to infect other people's souls. Satan is out to influence and control your soul. Your soul is where the spirit of the anti-christ wants to sit and dwell (II Thessalonians 2:4). Again your soul is your mind, emotions and will. This is where your self life is. Satan is out for himself only and wants to get you focused on yourself.

Some poisons are so deadly that just a little affects your entire body. Miriam's poison affected Aaron. Korah's poison affected the men around him. Some poisons are so deadly that they can quickly snuff the life right out of you. Learn to avoid them. Satan is out to remove God's oversight of your soul and to take the oversight of your soul. God's oversight has His life.

God's Word shows us what to do when someone is sowing distrust and disharmony.

> *Now I beseech you, brethren, mark them which cause divisions and offences contrary to the doctrine which ye have learned; and avoid them. For they that are such serve not our Lord Jesus Christ, but their own belly; and by good words and fair speeches deceive the hearts of the simple.*
>
> Romans 16:17-18

> *Finally, brethren, pray for us, that the word of the Lord may have free course, and be glorified, even as it is with you: and that we may be delivered from unreasonable and wicked men: for all men have not faith. But the Lord is faithful, who shall stablish you, and keep you from evil. And we have confidence in the Lord touching you, that ye both do and will do the things which we command you. And the Lord direct your hearts into the love of God, and into the patient waiting for Christ. Now we command you, brethren, in the name of our Lord Jesus Christ, that ye withdraw yourselves from every brother that walketh disorderly, and not after the tradition which he received of us. For yourselves know how ye ought to follow us: for we behaved not ourselves disorderly among you; neither did we eat any man's bread for nought; but wrought with labour and travail night and day, that we might not be chargeable to any of you: not because we have not power, but to make ourselves an ensample unto you to follow us. For even*

when we were with you, this we commanded you, that if any would not work, neither should eat. For we hear that there are some which walk among you disorderly, working not at all, but are busybodies. Now them that are such we command and exhort by our Lord Jesus Christ, that with quietness they work, and eat their own bread. But ye, brethren, be not weary in well doing. And if any man obey not our word by this epistle, note that man, and have no company with him, that he may be ashamed.

II Thessalonians 3:1-14

We are to *withdraw* ourselves from such people. They are dangerous to everyone. We don't play with fire. We don't play with poisonous adders. We don't play with nitroglycerin. And we shouldn't risk damaging our souls by listening to satan's servants. *Have no company with them.* Nothing could be more plain!

At one point, while crossing the wilderness, God told Moses to separate himself from the disobedient and rebellious people.

Separate yourselves from among this congregation, that I may consume them in a moment.

Numbers 16:21

We need to keep our distance from ungodly and disruptive elements. We must keep our family members and those of our spiritual family over whom we have been given authority. This is our responsibility as porters of the gate. Keep out what God wants kept out, and let in only what God wants let in.

When we are obedient to God's Word and walk in wisdom, God has promised that nothing will harm us. He Himself will *bruise satan under our feet shortly.*

For your obedience is come abroad unto all men. I am glad therefore on your behalf: but yet I would have you wise unto that which is good, and simple concerning evil. And the God of peace shall bruise Satan under your feet shortly. The grace of our Lord Jesus Christ be with you. Amen.
Romans 16:19-20

The benefits of unity in the Body of Christ are many. We should never lose sight of them.

Behold, how good and how pleasant it is for brethren to dwell together in unity! It is like the precious ointment upon the head, that ran down upon the beard, even Aaron's beard: that went down to the skirts of his garments; as the dew of Hermon, and as the dew that descended upon the mountains of Zion: for there the Lord commanded the blessing, even life for evermore.
Psalm 133:1-3

When we dwell in unity, God can pour His precious ointment, or anointing, down upon us, and it will flow down to every part of the Body. Satan will do anything to prevent that from happening. Satan's main way to stop God's influence is to take the oversight of your soul.

It is to our benefit to avoid the evil influences that may threaten our souls and those of our Church, family and friends. This is *the porter principle*.

Chapter 8

The Bishop Ministry

Now the God of peace, that brought again from the dead our Lord Jesus, that great shepherd of the sheep, through the blood of the everlasting covenant, make you perfect in every good work to do His will, working in you that which is wellpleasing in His sight, through Jesus Christ; to whom be glory for ever and ever. Amen.

Hebrews 13:20-21

The plan of God for each of us is glorious. His desire is to make us *perfect in every good work*. One of the ministries we need restored to the Church to bring about that desired perfection is that of the bishop. Until now, most churches have believed that the word *bishop* is synonymous with *shepherd* and *pastor*. This is only a partial truth. The bishop ministry and the shepherding ministry are separate and distinct.

Shepherding is a serious business—as we have come to realize in recent decades. The bishop ministry, however, has been shunted aside and given a lower place of importance, as if shepherding were everything. The concept of the true bishop is yet to be restored to the Church with the importance that God intended. This ministry has been so neglected that many of those who have come into the move of the Spirit in recent years have not even heard of a bishop, let alone known what his duties are.

Many good pastors have the heart of a shepherd and perform well in that role. They are faithful caretakers of the flock. Most, however, have not yet received the revelation of the bishoping aspect of the ministry, while others have not been willing to accept the responsibilities involved. Few have risen to the authority necessary to the bishop's ministry.

Bishops are ordained by God to rule over your soul. They are not called to lord over your spirit or soul. Only Jesus is Lord. But Jesus has established bishops to oversee His people while they are here on the earth. He establishes bishops for our good.

> *For rulers are not a terror to good works, but to the evil. Wilt thou then not be afraid of the power* [authority]? *do that which is good, and thou shalt have praise of the same: for he is the minister of God to thee for good. But if thou do that which is evil, be afraid; for he beareth not the sword in vain: for he is the minister of God, a revenger to execute wrath upon him that doeth evil.*
>
> Romans 13:3-4

Some movements, which have emphasized the close, personal shepherding of the flock, have become extreme in some regards.

We are all Christians. Not one of us is ordained to reign over his brothers. Not one of us is ordained to make decisions on his own, apart from the leading of the Spirit of God and the Word of God.

Many of the groups which have fallen into these abuses are led by teachers who are not qualified to lay foundations, to give proper setting to their teachings, or to expound the true meaning of God's Word—by revelation. The Church needs people of a deeper calling and experience, those the Bible calls *apostles and prophets.*

> *And are built upon the foundation of the apostles and prophets, Jesus Christ Himself being the chief corner stone;*
>
> Ephesians 2:20

An example of one such teaching is that of the twelfth chapter of First Corinthians. Most doma teachers would say that this is a teaching about *spiritual gifts.*

> *Now concerning spiritual gifts, brethren, I would not have you ignorant.*
>
> I Corinthians 12:1

This opening phrase, however, in the original, reads: *concerning spirituals*. The Greek word used is *pneumatikos*, which means *a world of spiritual operations or matters*. There are many spiritual matters that are never touched upon. One of them is the fact that the operations of God come from the Father aspect, the administrations of God come through Jesus who administrates the five-fold ministry, and the manifestation and gift aspect come through the Holy Spirit, the Manifestor who brings all of God's operations and administrations to pass. Another is the order established by God for these *spirituals.*

> *And God hath set some in the church, first apostles, secondarily prophets, thirdly teachers, after that miracles, then gifts of healings, helps, governments, diversities of tongues.*
> I Corinthians 12:28

Pneumatikos does not mean spiritual gifts inherent in born-again Christians. *Pneumatikos* is not the same as *charismas*. It is not *the direct intervention of God through His people*, or *phanerosis*, the word used in verse 7 for manifestation.

> *But the manifestation of the Spirit is given to every man to profit withal.*
> I Corinthians 12:7

Pneumatikos includes both. It includes all spiritual matters and workings.

The word *gifts*, of First Corinthians 12 in the King James Version of the Bible, is italicized, showing that it was added by the translators with the hope of clarifying the passage. By adding the word *gifts* here, they succeeded only in further clouding the issue. Paul was talking here about the whole realm of spiritual matters, not just spiritual manifestations.

The word used here in verse 7 for *manifestation* is *phanerosis*. It speaks of *God making Himself visible by operating in some direct and specific way that does not usually occur*: things like words of wisdom and knowledge, miracles or healings. *Phanerosis* is a manifestation of God Himself, not of a person, that mostly occur through His people.

The word *charismas*, translated *spiritual gifts*, is used here in verse 4 and also in Romans 12.

> *Now there are diversities of gifts, but the same Spirit.*
> I Corinthians 12:4

Having then gifts differing according to the grace that is given to us, whether prophecy, let us prophesy according to the proportion of faith;

Romans 12:6

This word refers to spiritual faculties operating in believers: charisma, gifts of mercy, service, giving, ruling, and the like (Romans 12:6-8). This is such a vast subject that it could fill a book of its own. Here, I only want to show the difference between getting a revelation and seeing the whole foundation upon which the revelation is based. A close look at the Greek reveals the inaccuracies of many of the present-day teachings on this all-important subject.

In regard to shepherding, what most teachers have left out is the aspect of the true bishop ministry. Jesus is described as being both *the Shepherd and Bishop of your souls* (I Peter 2:25). The two roles are not identical. They are not one and the same. To shepherd is one thing; to bishop is something much more serious.

We need more true apostles in the Church today, those who have the vision and revelation and authority to perform well in the role of bishop.

An apostle is one who at different times manifests all the five-fold ministry or the five facets of Jesus. Apostles are sent from God to the people. The word *apostle* means *one who is sent*. A man does not decide to be an apostle, just as a man does not decide to be a prophet, teacher, pastor or evangelist. God takes hold of him and sets him in that position. Apostles are arrested, appointed, and approved by God and then set or deposited where God wants them. Theirs is not an easy job.

The porter ministry can be manifested more clearly through the ministry of an apostle because the very call of the Lord upon his life is a crying out for order. Porterage is order. However, God does use prophets and pastors in the role also. God can use any of the five-fold ministry as such if He needs to as the need arises. However, an apostle functions in the anointing of order all the time.

Bishops set things in order wherever they go. This is important because, when we are not in God's order, we limit what He can do in the midst of us. When things are set in proper order, God is free to work as He desires.

The importance of the apostle does not negate the close relationship of the rest of the five-fold ministry to God, nor does it discount His speaking to them. But apostles bring order, and true portering is possible only when a body of believers is willing to come into alignment under the mighty hand of Father God and when someone is present to impose that order. In a properly ordered atmosphere, every member of the Body can function properly.

The elders of the New Testament were far more than most of us realize. These mature and godly men were full-time ministers to the flock. They were not men who sat around in board meetings. They were shepherds and bishops of God's people.

If we take the bishoping aspect out of order and place it under the cloak of shepherding, we guarantee that the bishop ministry will have no power to operate effectively, and that it will never get the attention it deserves.

Anytime a revelation of God is not received through the proper channel or order, it gets distorted. Invariably something vital is passed over. The revelation of the bishop's mantle cannot come forth effectively through the shepherd's cloak or through the revelation of a shepherd.

The set-man or pastor is called to both shepherd and bishop his flock. The two roles are not the same, however. The word for pastor is *poimen, one who shepherds the flock.* The word for bishop, however, is *episkopos, one who takes the oversight of the soul.* We need both these ministries.

The Hebrew word, used in the Old Testament for *shepherd,* is *raah,* meaning *to tend a flock, to feed, associate with as a friend; pastor.* It also has another meaning, showing us the qualities of the pastor in the realm of bishop. In this sense, it means *to rule, break and devour, to shear.*

So, the New Testament word for *bishop* is *episkopos, a superintendent, an officer in general charge of a church, an overseer, one who takes the oversight.* This word comes from the word *episkopeo* which means *to look diligently, to beware, take the oversight.*

In the recent past, because shepherds did not wait for the full restoration of the bishoping ministry, they had to use force to keep their sheep in line, instead of possessing the true authority of the bishop. The truth is seen in God's order for marriage (Ephesians 5:21-33).

The responsibility of the husband, who would be a qualified head, is to manifest agape love. That love will enable him to be both authoritative and considerate, firm and caring. The same applies to a set-man. In order for genuine authority to operate in the Body, the set-man must be possessed of a godly love that makes him function in a Christ-like way. From this Christ-like conduct emanates his authority to function as a true bishop over the flock.

The correct order of the Body, with the corresponding authority, can be restored only by apostles and prophets. We desperately need true apostles and prophets who will restore the proper foundations to the Church and give us something solid on which to build. Only then can the ministry of bishops be fully appreciated and applied. When we try to build on shaky foundations, the results are tragic. How can they be otherwise?

Just as it was in the days of the first apostles, today's apostles are given the revelation of divine governing order. This does not mean that they are lords or dictators. It means that they hear God's voice and lay for us the correct foundational truths on which we can build the Body of Christ on earth.

Many people have tried to use God's Word out of context and misapplied, and it simply doesn't work. When we are living in obedience to God's Word and are placed in proper order, things begin to happen for our benefit.

Some people are proclaiming half-truths. That doesn't produce results either. A half-truth produces the *spirit of error* (see First John 4:6). We need the full and complete truth in order to build a proper house. Only knowing the complete truth will make us free.

And ye shall know the truth, and the truth shall make you free.

John 8:32

The Pharisees often listened to the teachings of Jesus. They could never understand what He was saying, however, because they were interpreting His words by a surface revelation. And these were brilliant and well-educated men. Every teaching mantle must come under an apostolic foundational mantle.

The truth actually sounded offensive to the learned Jews of Jesus' days. When He told them the truth, they wanted to kill Him.

But now ye seek to kill Me, a man that hath told you the truth, which I have heard of God: this did not Abraham.
John 8:40

Truth is not always pleasant. It is not always what we want to hear. Becoming so hardened to the truth that we only want to hear what sounds good to us, however, is very dangerous.

Our concept of the bishop ministry, fostered by the political office of bishop existing in many churches, is that a bishop rules over other ministers or other works. This is not the biblical application of the word. A bishop is responsible primarily for his flock. This does not omit the fact that are God-called and God-prepared men of God who serve as spiritual fathers to the other five-fold ministry and sometimes to the churches of other five-fold men. A true spiritual father does not try to reign over other men of God, but desires to help, encourage, bring clarity, guide and be a friend to them. This is true spiritual covering that also points out error for the purpose of helping these men.

Feed the flock of God which is among you, taking the oversight thereof, not by constraint, but willingly; not for filthy lucre, but of a ready mind; neither as being lords over God's heritage, but being ensamples to the flock.
I Peter 5:2-3

Because many still think of the bishop in the sense of the office of bishop (as known in the liturgical churches), many Christians still reject the office of bishop altogether. We must change this dangerous attitude. A true bishop is more than a title with religious garb to accompany it.

Taking the oversight of the soul of a man is the bishop ministry, *the porter principle*. Again, it is not lording over the individual. If we are lording over a person, we will overrule, not rule over.

> *Remember them which have the rule over you, who have spoken unto you the word of God: whose faith follow, considering the end of their conversation.*
>
> Hebrews 13:7

The Greek word translated *rule* here is *hegeomai* and means *to lead or command with official authority, to deem or consider, account, be chief and governor, judge, and to have the rule over*. It comes from a word meaning *to lead, to bring or drive, induce, carry and keep, bring forth, lead away, be open*.

The New Testament word for *lord* is *katakurieuo, to control, subjugate, exercise dominion over*.

In too many Christian circles, the people are submitting themselves, not to the Spirit of Christ, but to the opinions of men. Some leaders want to take the place of Jesus and become Lord over their followers, projecting themselves into every decision of daily life. They don't want to leave any decision with the individual. They tell their flock what to do and when to do it: for example, what car to buy. This is not oversight, but lordship. The bishop ministry takes the oversight of another person's soul through the Spirit of Christ.

A true bishop approves truth and puts a stop to error. A true bishop confirms what God has placed in the heart of another person, while weeding out that which has been sown by satan, self, the flesh and the world. He proves that which is *good, and acceptable, and perfect.*

> *And be not conformed to this world: but be ye transformed by the renewing of your mind, that ye may prove what is that good, and acceptable, and perfect, will of God.*
> Romans 12:2

By protecting God's people from the evil desires of satan, the bishop enables us to move forward toward our divine destiny. The bishop, then, is God's gift to the Church, His assigned porter at the gates of our souls.

A true bishop can sense in the Spirit those things that are holding you back from receiving all that God has for you. He can help you overcome hindrances to those blessings.

It is a shame that the roles of shepherd and bishop have been lost or distorted in the Church. Should the Church wonder why they are experiencing such leanness of spirit these days? Much of the Church has lost God's order in the Church. Unless we see a restoration of this vital ministry in the Church today, the Body of Christ cannot become properly aligned. Until the Church is willing to have bishops over them in the Lord, the Church will not receive many of the greater things the Lord has prepared.

Rejecting the bishops that God has placed over you is rejecting Him as Bishop of our souls. He oversees your souls through His set-men. How can He return to a Church that rejects Him as Lord of their lives?

"For ye were as sheep going astray; but are now returned unto the Shepherd and Bishop of your souls (*psuche*)." (I Peter 2:25)

Whom the heaven must receive until the times of restitution of all things, which God hath spoken by the mouth of all His holy prophets since the world began.

Acts 3:21

This word *restitution* comes from *apokathistemi* which means *to reconstitute in health, home and organization.*

The *restitution of all things,* spoken of here, certainly includes the state of the Church, which is our spiritual family that is made up of domestic families. The condition of the Church is preventing the return of our Lord. We need bishops to restore us to proper spiritual condition.

Some of the responsibilities of the bishop are not popular. The apostle Paul wrote to Timothy:

Preach the word; be instant in season, out of season; reprove, rebuke, exhort with all longsuffering and doctrine.

II Timothy 4:2

Timothy was commissioned to guard the people under him from false doctrine. Bishops not only reveal false doctrines: they reveal wrong attitudes; they reveal pride; they reveal hidden sins; they reveal personal faults that can cause certain people to lose their right standing and true destiny with God. In doing this, a true bishop leads his people to repentance toward Christ.

The caring and comforting role of the shepherd must be tempered by the more forceful role of the bishop. Love and discipline are not mutually exclusive. If you love, you discipline. A good pastor will do both.

When a pastor loves his flock, he doesn't hesitate to eliminate anything that threatens their safety. Feeding them and leading them to green pastures and water is not his total duty. Sheep are often oblivious to dangers. The shepherd must take upon himself the role of guarding and protecting and ridding the sheep of anything that endangers their well-being. For the most part, they cannot do that for themselves.

When we love people, how can we not address the delicate issues that threaten their future? How can we look the other way? How can we avoid conflict? Is our duty to be liked? Or is it to look out for the welfare of the sheep?

Parents have to make some unpopular decisions for their children. Teachers have to make some unpopular decisions in the classroom. Good government officials have to make some unpopular decisions for their electorate. And those who are willing to receive the bishop's mantle must be willing to make some hard and unpopular decisions—for the good of the entire Body.

The Scriptures reveal that the leadership of the Church is a gift from God for its benefit, not an imposition upon it. The ministries of shepherd and bishop should be received in this spirit in which it is offered. God is not trying to rob me of the joy of life. He is trying to release me to true joy.

Your response to your assigned under-shepherd and under-bishop should be willing obedience and submission, for he has been placed as God's representative to do for you what God wants done in your life. He is responsible both for your nurturing and for the correction of your soul. Don't make his job impossible through rebellion and disdain of his authority.

On one hand, the shepherd must be loving and gentle with the sheep. We get a picture of his devotion to the flock from Isaiah.

> *He shall feed His flock like a shepherd: He shall gather the lambs with His arm, and carry them in His bosom, and shall gently lead those that are with young.*
>
> Isaiah 40:11

Not only does he feed them and lead them to water, he actually carries them. From the original, we understand that he is *to lift, accept, and bear them up, bring them forth and advance them.* The word also means *desire, ease, marry, receive, and wear.* He has them in his bosom. He actually wears the flock. They become part of his being: bone of his bone and flesh of his flesh.

He further shows his love and devotion by trying to see that their every need is met. If they are wounded, he patiently nurses them back to health. He risks his own life to protect them from predators, to find them or send out a search party when they have gone astray, and to rescue them when they are in danger and cannot help themselves. Because of this demonstration of love and devotion to their welfare, they love and trust him explicitly.

The ministry of the shepherd and bishop rests firmly on this foundation of godly love and concern. People respond to love. And loving discipline is not resented.

Many Christians have readily embraced the idea of the pastor as shepherd. Their thoughts are of the benefits described in David's famous Psalm.

> *The Lord is my shepherd; I shall not want. He maketh me to lie down in green pastures: He leadeth me beside the still waters. He restoreth my soul: He leadeth me in the paths of righteousness for His name's sake. Yea, though I walk through the valley of the shadow of death, I will fear no*

evil: for Thou art with me; Thy rod and Thy staff they comfort me. Thou preparest a table before me in the presence of mine enemies: Thou anointest my head with oil; my cup runneth over. Surely goodness and mercy shall follow me all the days of my life: and I will dwell in the house of the Lord for ever.

Psalm 23

We all like to be sheltered and nurtured, guarded in trouble and led in tranquility through peaceful places. But there are some other aspects of the shepherding role (that of discipline, for example), that we don't find as pleasant.

A bishop is like a scout or a sentry, diligently regarding all the aspects of your soul, willingly taking the oversight of your welfare. Jesus is Lord of your being, but He has placed His bishops to keep watch over your soul, to guide and correct you, as a parent does a child, for its own good and protection.

We must accept Jesus as both Shepherd and Bishop of our souls, "For ye were as sheep going astray; but are now returned unto the *Shepherd* (*poimen*-Shepherd) and *Bishop* (*episkopos*-Overseer) of your souls (*psuche*-mind, emotions, will)" (I Peter 2:25), and we must accept His designated setmen as both shepherds and bishops, "*Feed* (*poimen*-Shepherd) the flock of God which is among you, *taking the oversight* (*episkopeo*-take the oversight, to oversee) thereof..." (I Peter 5:2). We cannot afford to resent it when a concerned leader confronts us with whatever is wrong in our souls and sets out to correct it.

The local flock of God needs bishops. The city needs bishops. And the region needs bishops. Anointed men of

God must close every door to satan and open every door to Jesus. Together, we must drive away the enemy and welcome our Lord with open arms. This is *the porter principle*.

Chapter 9

Restoring the Bishop Ministry

Therefore the redeemed of the Lord shall return, and come with singing unto Zion; and everlasting joy shall be upon their head: they shall obtain gladness and joy; and sorrow and mourning shall flee away.

Isaiah 51:11

It is time for a return to Zion. Understanding the reasons that the bishop ministry has been neglected might help us to see how we can restore it. Often identification of the problem is half the solution.

The first reason that many are not contending for the bishop ministry is ignorance. Most people don't have the revelation of what a bishop is or what his work is. We need a foundational revelation.

My people are destroyed for lack of knowledge: because thou hast rejected knowledge, I will also reject thee, that thou shalt be no priest to Me: seeing thou hast forgotten the law of thy God, I will also forget thy children.

Hosea 4:6

The second reason we don't have bishops in our churches is the traditional (and often misleading) use of the term *bishop* in many churches to mean a political position. *Bishop* is far more than a title we give to elderly pastors. A true bishop is not a bishop by name only. He has assumed a demanding work, a ministry, an office.

This is a true saying, If a man desire the office of a bishop, he desireth a good work.

I Timothy 3:1

The word *work* here means *an act of toiling, a labour or deed*. The work of a bishop is the work of a porter. And, while the political position of *bishop* derives its authority from those making the appointment and from the title itself, the biblical bishop derives his authority directly from Heaven.

The third reason we don't have bishops in our churches is the misuse of the term in recent years by those involved in the several popular movements, who believed and taught that a bishop was simply a shepherd, nothing more. Many have been confused by this teaching and have simply thought that the office of bishop was irrelevant.

The final reason the Church does't have bishops today is that it has rebelled against the office of apostles.

We all appreciate the ministry of the evangelist. He brings the good news of salvation. Most appreciate the pastor, caretaker of the flock. The teacher is respected. He brings good information. The prophet, however, is much less recognized and welcomed. He might, after all, begin to speak things that cut to the heart and lay forth more of God's purpose for the Church. The apostle is the least received and welcomed of the five. He comes with God's divine order, and the Church doesn't much like that. It was true also in the first century.

> *For I think that God hath set forth us the apostles last, as it were appointed to death: for we are made a spectacle unto the world, and to angels, and to men.*
>
> I Corinthians 4:9

The word *spectacle* also means *theater, a place for a public show where everything on exhibit can be closely scrutinized and perceived in its entirely.* Once Jesus has successfully restored the office of apostle to the Church, the office of bishop will soon follow. The prophetic ministry of a true prophet should set the stage for apostolic ministry since a prophet also is a foundational office.

Having identified the problems, we must say that the first step in restoring the ministry of bishops to the Church is restoring our allegiance to the true Bishop, Jesus. As long as we are not totally submitted to His will for our lives and totally committed to cooperate with the leadership He provides, we will never have the true apostolic ministry in the Church.

For too long, much of the Church has looked to the Lord selfishly, only using Him to provide their physical and material needs. Many Christians know only the final part of First Peter 2:24: *by whose stripes ye were healed.* This has become a favorite portion of Scripture for millions. Healing is always a popular subject. Other parts of the chapter, however, which deal with submission, obedience and order, are not nearly as popular.

Healing is important, and God wants to heal His people. If we get ourselves in proper order, healing can be released—along with many other physical and material blessings. It is wrong, however, to focus on physical benefits before we deal with the root cause of our problems, our rebellion against God and His order. Let's face it. The Body of Christ is out of order. We must return to Christ, the Shepherd and Bishop of our souls.

> *For ye were as sheep going astray; but are now returned unto the Shepherd and Bishop of your souls.*
> I Peter 2:25

The word used for *astray* is *planao*. It means *roaming away from safety, truth, or virtue*. This is a dangerous pursuit. We must reverse this course and turn back to the One who truly loves us and knows what is best for us.

If we gladly accept the other pastoral aspects of Jesus' ministry to us, why is it that we cannot accept Him as Bishop? How is it that we can pray without shame, "Jesus, heal me; Jesus, touch me; Jesus, bless me; Jesus, prosper me," and yet not be willing to submit to His closer scrutiny of our lives?

The answer has to be that many believers' self life rebels against submission to the will of God. The soul wants to continue in soulish activity: selfishness, rebellion, insubordination, and disorder. Let us return whole-heartedly to Jesus.

The second step to restoring the ministry of bishops is a return to mutual submission in the Body of Christ and the willingness to learn from others. The first Book of Peter contains a teaching on mutual submission for husbands and wives, which also serves as a general exhortation and expression of a church in order and unity. It concludes in this way:

> *Finally, be ye all of one mind, having compassion one of another, love as brethren, be pitiful, be courteous:*
> I Peter 3:8

Much of the Church is very far from this idyllic unity and love for one another. The Church in general has much to do and a long way to go. Our goal must be perfect alignment with Christ and perfect alignment with His Body. Once we come under Christ properly, we must make every effort to develop mutual submission.

Not everyone responds well to the work of the bishop. The Word of God admonishes us:

And ye have forgotten the exhortation which speaketh unto you as unto children, My son, despise not thou the chastening of the Lord, nor faint when thou art rebuked of Him:
Hebrews 12:5

The response the Lord is looking for from us is a willing submission to His correction. The response He usually gets is very different. The word *despise* is from the Greek word meaning *to disesteem, have little regard for*. The word *faint* is from a word meaning *dissolve or break up*. When you are rebuked by a bishop, your soul or self may want to despise the person who is doing the rebuking. Your love for the set-man may grow dim. That need not be the case.

When you realize that it is the Lord who is doing the rebuking and that He is doing it because He loves you, it enables you to realize that you will benefit from a proper response to the rebuke. This should bring about a greater realization in you of God's great love for you. It can make you love and respect your set-man even more. If you honor God, it is not difficult to honor God's man.

Let the elders that rule well be counted worthy of double honour, especially they who labour in the word and doctrine. For the scripture saith, Thou shalt not muzzle the

> *ox that treadeth out the corn. And, The labourer is worthy of his reward.*
>
> I Timothy 5:17-18

These men are *worthy of double honour.* They are to be esteemed very highly *for their work's sake.*

> *And we beseech you, brethren, to know them which labour among you, and are over you in the Lord, and admonish you; and to esteem them very highly in love for their work's sake. And be at peace among yourselves.*
>
> I Thessalonians 5:12-13

We, on the other hand, feel uncomfortable about the very close work God desires to do through His servants. God's bishop teaches and preaches the Word of God that divides you asunder in soul and spirit. This dividing asunder is for the purpose of realigning and readjusting your soul or self life and then putting them back together so you can live in right standing and peace. The dividing asunder of your joints and marrow speak of the need for some to be dislocated in the Body and placed in their true calling. Some are trying to operate in God's Body out of their calling.

> *For the word of God is quick, and powerful, and sharper than any twoedged sword, piercing even to the dividing asunder of soul and spirit, and of the joints and marrow, and is a discerner of the thoughts and intents of the heart. Neither is there any creature that is not manifest in His sight: but all things are naked and opened unto the eyes of Him with whom we have to do.*
>
> Hebrews 4:12-13

Comfortable or not, the Word of God clearly teaches us to submit to one another in humility.

> *Likewise, ye younger, submit yourselves unto the elder. Yea, all of you be subject one to another, and be clothed with humility: for God resisteth the proud, and giveth grace to the humble. Humble yourselves therefore under the mighty hand of God, that He may exalt you in due time:*
>
> I Peter 5:5-6

Rebelling against God's ordained order is dangerous. God resists the proud. He gives grace to the humble. He wants to exalt each of us, but He demands that we first humble ourselves in order to be exalted.

God has placed His servants very carefully in the Body. He has a very precise plan about how they are to operate and what they are to accomplish. He has done all this because of His great love for each of us.

He very carefully places you in a body under a true set-man who will faithfully serve as shepherd and bishop of your soul. He knows where you will do best. Your assigned place may not be the easiest, but it will be the best.

While it is true that reading and studying the Word of God can help you submit to Him as Bishop, that is not enough. You must also submit to His order and to those who are specifically called and anointed to speak His words.

If you are willing to come under the set-man God has placed as porter of your soul, you will grow and become a mature and responsible individual. If not, you are in great danger.

Much of the Church is very accustomed to pastors and teachers who encourage and build them up, but many are still resisting oversight. What are you afraid of? God will not harm you in any way. His will is always best. Many of us still resent it when someone takes authority and deals with our selfish and rebellious attitudes and lifestyles. But it must be done—whether we like it or not.

The third step in the restoration of the bishop ministry is bringing to maturity men who will be capable and willing to accept such a great responsibility. Peter, in teaching the early church about the need for oversight, used the phrase, *taking the oversight thereof.* This oversight has to be taken or seized with authority. Not many are bold enough to do the seizing.

Paul was an apostle and a senior bishop and had the authority to appoint other bishops. He prepared both Timothy and Titus for this office. Timothy was the first bishop ordained to Ephesus. Titus was ordained as the bishop of Crete.

> *For this cause left I thee in Crete, that thou shouldest set in order the things that are wanting, and ordain elders in every city, as I had appointed thee:*
>
> **Titus 1:5**

We desperately need more mature apostles who can do this work and raise others up to do it, as well.

When we return to Jesus and to His appointed men, healing, anointing, and God's wonderful workings will become a normal part of our everyday life. When we are properly aligned within the Body of Christ, God will be able to do, with ease, all that He desires.

Let us turn to Him today and live.

> *Turn, O backsliding children, saith the Lord; for I am married unto you: and I will take you one of a city, and two of a family, and I will bring you to Zion:*
>
> **Jeremiah 3:14**

He will do this through His appointed servants. This is *the porter principle.*

Chapter 10

Taming the Wild Ass

For vain man would be wise, though man be born like a wild ass's colt.

Job 11:12

As we have seen, the soul requires a porter. It is easily influenced and will follow either Jesus or satan. God has set earthly porters, His set-men, to guard your souls, to nourish and correct them.

The creation of man is a powerful expression of God's intended order for the entire sphere of creation. Man has a God-given position that no other creature can fill. His makeup explains God's purpose in placing porters on the earth. He made everything to reproduce *after its own kind.*

> *And God said, Let the earth bring forth grass, the herb yielding seed, and the fruit tree yielding fruit after his kind, whose seed is in itself, upon the earth: and it was so. And the earth brought forth grass, and herb yielding seed after*

his kind, and the tree yielding fruit, whose seed was in itself, after his kind: and God saw that it was good.

            Genesis 1:11-12

Everything that God created reproduced *after its own kind*. Flowers do not produce cattle. And plant seeds do not hatch into chicks. Everything that God made reproduces after its kind. Spirit brings forth spirit, and soul brings forth soul—just as surely as dogs give birth to puppies.

God's first order of creation was the *body kind*, meaning the plant realm. All grass, trees, herbs, and other plants were created after their own kind. They have neither soul nor spirit.

God's second order of creation was the *soul* or *dualistic kind*, the animal realm. All creatures of the animal kingdom have a body and a soul: horses, dogs, cats, cattle, etc. In Genesis 1:24-25 we see them described as *living creature(s)*.

And God said, Let the earth bring forth the living creature after his kind, cattle, and creeping thing, and beast of the earth after his kind: and it was so. And God made the beast of the earth after his kind, and cattle after their kind, and every thing that creepeth upon the earth after his kind: and God saw that it was good.

            Genesis 1:24-25

The Hebrew word translated *living* is *chay*, and it means *alive, raw, appetite, strong, and beast*. It carries the connotation of *freshness and wild vitality*. The word for *creature* is *nephesh*. This is the same word translated elsewhere as *soul*, and it means *a breathing creature with a will, a mind, and desires*. It also means *greedy and discontented, jeopardy, and lust*.

And the Lord God formed man of the dust of the ground, and breathed into his nostrils the breath of life; and man became a living soul.

Genesis 2:7

Man also has a soul. This word *nephesh* is the Hebrew parallel for the Greek word *psuche*, used in the New Testament for *soul*. Again, it denotes *the mind, the emotions, and the will*. The soul is vital and strong and wants its own way, but God has given no authority to the soul of any creature.

God's third order of creation was the *tripartite kind*: that which is made up of spirit, soul, and body; man, made in God's image.

And God said, Let Us make man in Our image, after Our likeness:

Genesis 1:26

When God decided to create man in His own image and likeness, He determined that man would be modeled and fashioned to resemble Himself. The Hebrew word for *image* also means *shape, like, similitude, and manner*. God's image is spirit, soul, and body—as we see throughout the Bible.

God has a soul: mind, emotions, and will. He can experience desire, anger, sorrow, and love, etc.

God has a body. Moses saw His back sides. God writes with His finger. We are in His hand. His eyes run *to and fro*. All things ultimately will be under His feet. And more.

But God rules by the spirit portion of His being. Our whole being is to be spirit-ruled, as well.

God is a Spirit: and they that worship Him must worship Him in spirit and in truth.

John 4:24

God's third order of creation was intended to have dominion over the first and second. The tripartite beings were set in order to bring the other realms under control or subjection, to place them under the yoke, to tread them down, and to conquer and rule.

And God said...let them have dominion over the fish of the sea, and over the fowl of the air, and over the cattle, and over all the earth, and over every creeping thing that creepeth upon the earth.

And God blessed them, and God said unto them, Be fruitful, and multiply, and replenish the earth, and subdue it: and have dominion over the fish of the sea, and over the fowl of the air, and over every living thing that moveth upon the earth.

Genesis 1:26, 28

God was telling man: You take dominion over the soulish realm. Take dominion over your own soul, over the souls of the animals, and over the soul of every living person. It is the spirit-man that has been given authority by God to rule over the animals, the plants, and over the souls of man. Spiritual man is to dominate the entire plant world, animal world, and the world of humans, as well.

Jesus proved His dominance over the animal kingdom when He mounted a donkey that had never been ridden before (Matthew 21:2-9; Mark 11:1-11), and rode it into Jerusalem. *Jerusalem* means *founded peaceful*. An ass that has never been ridden is wild, yet Jesus displayed total dominion over the beast. It did not give Him a moment's difficulty, but was docile and obedient.

...He (Jesus) sendeth forth two of His disciples,

...and saith unto them, Go your way into the village...ye shall find a colt tied, wheron never man sat; loose him, and bring him.

And they brought the colt to Jesus, and cast their garments on Him; and He (Jesus) sat upon Him.
Mark 11:1-2, 7

He did not conquer the animal by brute strength, as is so often the case in taming wild animals. The animal did not buck and kick until it was tired, then succumb to the strength and guile of the rider. The dominion Jesus held in the spirit realm allowed Him a victory without struggle. The animal was instantly calm. It offered Him no resistance.

As we have seen in Job, man is *born like a wild ass's colt.* The soul-man is just like a wild ass, untamed, unbridled, and wild. Our souls not only are out of control, they resist being brought under control. The soul must be tamed.

When Jesus entered Jerusalem that day, He did so as King.

Tell ye the daughter of Sion, Behold, thy King cometh unto thee, meek, and sitting upon an ass, and a colt the foal of an ass.
Matthew 21:5

As King, Jesus was in control. He had all authority. He was *meek*, yet He was powerful. The people who witnessed that event clearly felt the air charged with His power.

And a very great multitude spread their garments in the way; others cut down branches from the trees, and strawed them in the way. And the multitudes that went before, and that followed, cried, saying, Hosanna to the Son of David: Blessed is He that cometh in the name of the Lord; Hosanna in the highest.

> Matthew 21:8-9

He was clearly in charge. The men and women along Jerusalem's streets recognized it that day. There was no doubt in their minds. This Man had authority. They spread their garments in the way. They cut down branches from the trees and covered the ground where He would cross. They cried out their praises.

No one had gone before Jesus with a trumpet. No one had shouted that the King was coming. Without provocation, the crowd was moved to adulation. Not a word had to be spoken. Jesus was in charge. He had dominion over every soul. He was Lord and King.

We are not talking about Jesus as God. He was now in flesh, the God-man/Son of man, and was subject to all the human weaknesses and frailties, just as any other man.

For we have not an high priest which cannot be touched with the feeling of our infirmities; but was in all points tempted like as we are, yet without sin.

> Hebrews 4:15

Jesus is King. Let all the earth bow before Him.

That ass was *brought* to him (Matthew 21:7). The word for *brought* here is *ago*. It means *to be driven, brought forth, and made open*. The soul of man is born as a wild ass. It must be brought to Jesus. The method used to induce that wild animal to follow can only be imagined. The important thing is that someone was willing to obey Jesus and to bring the animal to Him.

Something made that animal sense what was happening. And something in the animal made it willing to surrender its will to another.

Just as the disciples placed their garments on the wild ass, and the people placed their garments in the way, there must be a laying down of all cumbersome religious garb, our empty traditions, our clinging to the former things, if we want to be used of the Lord in these days. Old garments are restrictive. Old garments hinder us. Let God give you some new garments. Everything we have must be laid at Jesus' feet. Don't hold back anything from the King.

When their garments were in place, the disciples *set* Jesus upon the beast (Matthew 21:7). That word *set* means *superimposed, settled and appointed.* Jesus should be superimposed upon your life. He should be settled as your Lord. He should be appointed as your King. He must rule.

Thank God for the great *multitude* that responded that day to King Jesus. Thank God for their joyous cries of *Hosanna.* That word is an exclamation of adoration, meaning *Oh, save*! Jesus came to save our wild souls from an untamed life and a sure death.

The crowd recognized Him as *the Son of David.* Again, the name *David* means *boiling love.* A Man of love came in authority and power to save His people from their sins. Hosanna!

Why did Jesus not ride into the city on a camel? I believe that He rode the wild ass that day to demonstrate to us that He has the power to tame the wild soul of man, that nothing —no character flaw, no temperament—is too difficult for Him. He is Lord and King over all. What a joyful moment it is when we yield control of our wild nature to King Jesus!

Today, Jesus is not entering our cities and towns in bodily form, sitting upon an animal. He has placed His set-men, His servants, in places of authority to watch for our souls and to take dominion over the wild attitudes and to subdue the earth.

Allow your soul to be brought into submission. God never intended for it to reign supreme. Give your spirit free reign, by suppressing your wild soul in Christ. Cooperate with those who would bring you to the feet of the Master for His use. Willingly and joyfully submit to *the porter principle.*

Chapter 11

The Porter Inside You

And what I say unto you I say unto all, Watch.
                                            Mark 13:37

When a child is first born, he/she is totally helpless. It must be watched over constantly. He/she must be fed, clothed, bathed, and given a nap. As that child develops, however, he/she is able to do more and more for himself/herself. Maturity is a wonderful thing!

If all goes well, the day will arrive when that child (now a young man or woman) will be able to fend for himself/herself in the world. This is God's plan for the soul of every individual, as well.

God has set porters in His House to care for and nourish the little ones. They don't know what is good for them yet. They run into the street. They eat dirty things. They make messes. They get into things they know nothing about. They are slow to take the proper rest. They need our help.

God didn't intend for this process to be never-ending, however. He expects these little ones to grow and to come to maturity. He expects them to be able, at some point, to care for themselves. It is even natural for Him to expect that they will eventually be capable of caring for others.

> *That we henceforth be no more children, tossed to and fro, and carried about with every wind of doctrine, by the sleight of men, and cunning craftiness, whereby they lie in wait to deceive; but speaking the truth in love, may grow up into Him in all things, which is the head, even Christ:*
> Ephesians 4:14-15

At some point, we expect children to *grow up*. After we have cared for them for many years, given them an example to live by, and taught them what is proper in life, it is time for them to show what they are capable of doing. If they don't grow up, we become worried. Lack of growth is not normal. It is, in fact, cause for alarm.

Just as it takes many tedious and dedicated years to properly raise children, we cannot expect people to grow up spiritually overnight. It doesn't happen. We must expect a long process of growth, during which the person will need much outside help. We can expect them to show signs of growth. And we can expect that, at some point, they will be ready to take on the responsibility for their own souls.

It is this slow, teaching and training process that we often neglect in the spiritual world. A child has to be taught how to tie his shoes. He must be taught how to eat properly. He must be taught how to play well with other children. He must be taught everything. He does not do anything by instinct, as animals do.

This is the reason that God has set leadership in the Church: to properly train His little ones. Once they are trained, they are capable of caring for themselves and others. The guarded become the guards. The taught become the teachers. The recipients of our care become the care-givers. Even the mature still have to periodically be under a bishop if they are working in a secular world.

But we cannot take anything for granted. Watchmen must be serious people. To them we entrust the welfare of ourselves and our families. They cannot be childish, immature, or lazy. This is serious business. David placed responsible people to be *keepers of the gates of the tabernacle, keepers of the entry, and porters of the door of the tabernacle of the congregation* (I Chronicles 9:19-21).

You have the potential to be one of those trusted keepers. You never begin by being given a grave responsibility over others. You must prove yourself first. You do that by keeping yourself well. You set a watch on all sides of your life and allow no intruders to come in.

Just as the ancient porters at the gates examined and screened every potential visitor before giving them entrance, and just as they turned away anything and anyone they deemed dangerous to the life of the city, you must do the same for your own life. Learn to recognize enemies, and make sure that none get in. Learn to recognize the tactics of satan and to overcome them.

Lest Satan should get an advantage of us: for we are not ignorant of his devices.
II Corinthians 2:11

Porters were not only stationed at the gates of the city and at the tabernacle; they also guarded the king's throne. Four porters were placed at the *causeway*, an outer entrance (paralleling the *sarx*, or physical, flesh body), and two at Parbar, (or the *psuche*, soul entrance.)

At Parbar westward, four at the causeway, and two at Parbar. These are the divisions of the porters among the sons of Kore, and among the sons of Merari.

I Chronicles 26:18-19

Westward comes from a word meaning *to give or be security*. A *causeway* was *a thoroughfare, a path or a staircase*. Those who were permitted to enter through the causeway and into the outer courts were met by two more porters who had to approve of their entry before they could approach the king's throne. The king had to be protected at all costs.

Two large doors led to the king's throne room. One very trusted and able porter stood at each door. To me, these two porters are like the anointing and the Word, like Spirit and Truth. They are safeguards that are virtually impossible for falsehood to bypass. Arm yourself with these invaluable and invincible weapons.

You can see why only a chosen few were placed in these responsible positions. The work of a porter demands seriousness and maturity. Immature and childish people need not apply here. This is the reason we cannot afford to bypass the apparatus God has placed in the Church for our development and perfection.

When we become rightly aligned within the Body, we need not worry about somebody noticing. It will be very apparent—to God and to man. And when that day arrives, God's glory will be restored among us in fulness.

When the Lord shall have washed away the filth of the daughters of Zion, and shall have purged the blood of Jerusalem from the midst thereof by the spirit of judgment, and by the spirit of burning. And the Lord will create upon every dwelling place of mount Zion, and upon her assemblies, a cloud and smoke by day, and the shining of a flaming fire by night: for upon all the glory shall be a defence.

Isaiah 4:4-5

What glorious things we have to look forward to. Let's hurry and grow up. Let us cooperate fully and joyfully with those who are set over us in the Lord. Let's do everything necessary to show the maturity of taking charge of our own souls and becoming a porter of our own gates. Let us be vigilant. Let us watch.

Those of us who are married and have children have a larger responsibility. We must guard the entrance to our marriage and the entrance to our home. We must keep out the thief. We must guard our wives and our children against the desires of the evil one. We must recognize his deceits and repel them.

None of us is immune to attack. Satan attacked the apostle Paul. He used *unreasonable and wicked men* to do it (II Thessalonians 3:2). He will attack you too. He will use unruly, *unreasonable and wicked men* to hinder your spiritual progress.

Some of our enemies are not as obvious. One of them is called by the writer of Hebrews *any root of bitterness* (Hebrews 12:15). Bitterness can be a deadly enemy, bringing discouragement and devastation to an individual or to a ministry. Once satan has filled your spirit with bitterness, he can easily attack your health or your finances. Guard against bitterness diligently.

When you take the decision to set a watch upon your soul, you effectively close the door to satan. He can no longer touch you.

> *We know that whosoever is born of God sinneth not; but he that is begotten of God keepeth himself, and that wicked one toucheth him not.*
>
> I John 5:18

This word *keepeth* carries the idea of *a fortress or full military lines, maintaining and preserving*. When you get serious about protecting your soul and become a good porter, satan is powerless against you. The word used here for *toucheth* denotes *to set on fire*. Satan intends to influence, take over and burn your soul. You can prevent it from happening. The purpose of *the porter principle* is not to develop a group of perpetual babies who constantly need to be fed and cared for. The purpose is to see boys and girls grow into men and women capable of overseeing the general welfare of their own souls—and the souls of others.

Jesus is our example. His soul resisted the death of the cross. He sweat drops of blood in the Garden of Gethsemane. He bled out His self-life. He didn't want to die; but, in the end, He submitted Himself to the will of His Father and went quietly to the cross. To be the Shepherd and Bishop of our souls, Jesus had to prove that He could keep Himself. By constantly and consistently giving Himself to the will of His Father, He gave the enemy no place in His life.

> *Hereafter I will not talk much with you: for the prince of this world cometh, and hath nothing in Me.*
>
> John 14:30

Jesus closed the door to the prince of this world. He shut out demonic activity before it had the chance to damage His soul. He effectively shut our worry, frustration, and anxiety. His life and ministry was a success because He knew His enemy and gave him no space.

When He and His disciples were crossing the Sea of Galilee one day, a terrible storm overtook them in the middle of the sea. The disciples were frightened, but Jesus went to sleep. The disciples allowed doubt and fear to enter their minds, but Jesus refused to allow anything to enter His mind which was not first sifted by the Word of God and checked by the Holy Spirit. He took dominion over the winds and waves and stilled them—with a word.

The ultimate goal of your life is to become a general porter of your own life and maybe mature enough to serve as a porter to others in the House of God. The most natural thing in life is for a child to grow up, marry, and have children of his own. We worry about people who are slow in maturing. It isn't normal. Something is wrong and needs to be corrected.

There is much to be done in the Kingdom. God needs you to grow up quickly, take control of your own life and that of your family members, then give yourself willingly to the oversight of your set-men, for each of you to mature as to help porter the souls of others who are beginning the same process through which you have already passed.

You can never hope to rule in any capacity in the House of God, however, if you cannot yet rule your own soul, your own household, or your own secular job.

Keep thy heart with all diligence; for out of it are the issues of life.

Proverbs 4:23

It all begins in the soul. Keep yours well. Protect your intellect from contamination. Protect your feelings from pollution. Be vigilant! Guard against every attack! The fruit that you produce cannot be better than the soul in which it originates.

> *O generation of vipers, how can ye, being evil, speak good things? for out of the abundance of the heart the mouth speaketh.*
>
> Matthew 12:34

Don't give satan space to come in.

> *Neither give place to the devil.*
>
> Ephesians 4:27

Just as the angels did to guard God's throne in Heaven, say to him, "No! You're not coming in here!" Do it with authority and power, and he will run from you.

> *Submit yourselves therefore to God. Resist the devil, and he will flee from you.*
>
> James 4:7

When you have learned to keep you own soul, God will restore to you the delights of Eden. You will walk and talk with Him in unrestricted liberty. And His great design for your life will be worked out.

Jesus is knocking on the door of your soul and spirit, and you have the power to let Him in. Satan is knocking on the door of your soul and life, and you have the power to keep him out. This is *the porter principle*.

Chapter 12

The Struggle Within

And the children struggled together within her...and the Lord said unto her, Two nations are in thy womb, and...two manner of people shall be separated from thy bowels; and the one people shall be stronger than the other people; and the elder shall serve the younger.

Genesis 25:22-23

We have seen how King Jesus is coming to take full dominion over the untamed souls of His people, the same way He rode the wild ass and her colt into Jerusalem. We've examined God's intended order of creation (spirit, soul, and body) and become aware of the rule and authority the spirit-man is supposed to have over the soul and the human nature.

In the born again man, there is a constant struggle for superiority between the soulish-man and the spirit-man. If you are not born-again, you are still dualistic in expression. Without redemption, you have a dead spirit.

It is only Jesus, through the salvation process, who can rejuvenate your dead spirit-man and give you new life. Without a living spirit, you may appear to be alive, but you can have no God-given authority or ability. Your life will be dominated entirely by the soulish realm. And, since the soul has no God-given dominion, you can never have life's fullest expression.

This word *born*, used by the apostle John, means *to procreate of the father, regenerate. Born again* means *bring into existence again, beget, reestablish on a new basis.* This is what God does with a formerly dead spirit in a man who becomes born-again.

> *That which is born of the flesh is flesh; and that which is born of the Spirit is spirit. Marvel not that I said unto thee, Ye must be born again.*
>
> John 3:6-7

Because Adam and Eve were created in the image of God, they were intended to be ruled by the spirit. They were given dominion over the earth and all it contained. God's plan did not include satan's intrusion into the garden. God intended for Adam to exercise his dominion and protect himself and his family. Through what happened to them, however, it is clear that even godly people can be wrongly influenced and that, when the soulish realm dominates, destruction follows.

The proper choices for Adam and for Eve should have been clear. They had only one correct option. Their thinking became clouded, however, when they allowed their soulish realm to dominate their decision-making. The results were tragic. Adam and Eve "blew it" and fell from their exalted state.

We cannot afford, even for a minute, to allow the soul to take control of our lives. We cannot afford, as parents, to allow soulish activity to dominate our children. We cannot afford, as married people, to allow soulish activity to dominate our marriage. We cannot afford to miss God's best for our lives.

We have clearly seen that if the soul is not fully submitted to God and to His will for our lives, we open ourselves to the influence of satan and his evil desires for us. This conflict of soul and spirit produces the constant battle that we all face within. Our soul and spirit struggles within much as Esau and Jacob struggled within the womb of Rebekah.

And the children struggled together within her;
Genesis 25:22

Struggle means *break or bruise, discourage or oppress.* The soul and the spirit wrestle in violent warfare.

In the case of Rebekah, there were two nations struggling in her womb.

And the Lord said unto her, Two nations are in thy womb, and two manner of people shall be separated from thy bowels; and the one people shall be stronger than the other people; and the elder shall serve the younger.
Genesis 25:23

In the same way that Rebekah had two nations struggling within, there are two very different and very opposed forces within every born-again believer. We might actually say that there are two people struggling inside you. Those two people are represented by the *pneumatikos, those led by the spirit,* and the *psuchikos, those led by the soul.*

The word *separated* here has a connotation of a New Testament word which is *merismose,* which means *a dividing asunder.* Two sorts of people would be divided, severed and sundered, from the womb, or the belly, and one would take dominion.

There is a natural man, and there is a spiritual man.

And so it is written, The first man Adam was made a living soul; the last Adam was made a quickening spirit. Howbeit that was not first which is spiritual, but that which is natural; and afterward that which is spiritual.
                                I Corinthians 15:45-46

The natural man, or the *psuchikos*, is the firstborn, the eldest (since we first have a natural, physical birth). The birth of the soul and the flesh with it is always prior to a spiritual birth. When man is born, he is unregenerate, and he is a dualistic creature. The spirit man inside him is dead until and unless he is rejuvenated by Christ.

The natural man acts like the animals. He is motivated by the soulish realm and is subject to the desires and devices of the *psuche*, the soul.

The second birth Christ offers brings into being the *pneumatikos*, the spirit life. This spirit life comes second, and is the *younger* part of our being. Yet it is this younger portion of our beings that must take control, just as Esau had to become subservient to Jacob. It is only in this way that we can come into proper alignment with God. For He is Spirit, and He originally created us to be ruled by our spirits—not by our soulish ways.

These two kinds of realms are so different that it is a mistake to yoke them together, unless they are operating in harmony. The soul must come in harmony with the born-again spirit.

Be ye not unequally yoked together with unbelievers: for what fellowship hath righteousness with unrighteousness? and what communion hath light with darkness?
                                II Corinthians 6:14

It is wrong for Christian people to marry the unregenerate. Such a union cannot be blessed. It is a union of light and darkness, of truth and lie, of good and evil. Nothing good can come of it. Those who refuse to heed this scriptural admonition are only inviting tragedy into their lives.

Being born-again, however, does not isolate you from life's struggles. You still have those two forces warring within. Each wants to dominate the other. The soul is always persecuting the spirit and pressuring it to yield to evil.

But as then he that was born after the flesh persecuted him that was born after the Spirit, even so it is now.
Galatians 4:29

The soul of man is still rebellious and stubborn. It is still prone to passion and failure. It must be constantly kept under control.

This I say then, Walk in the Spirit, and ye shall not fulfil the lust of the flesh [sarx-human nature] For the flesh [sarx-human nature] lusteth against the Spirit, and the Spirit against the flesh: and these are contrary the one to the other: so that ye cannot do the things that ye would.
Galatians 5:16-17

God ordained that the elder would serve the younger, that the spirit would control the soul. In the case of Esau and Jacob, the fulfillment of God's plan was not immediately apparent. For many years it seemed that Esau and his family would prevail over Jacob and his descendants. Only time showed that God's chosen would prevail. As Jacob continued to grow and develop, everything came to light.

> *(For the children being not yet born, neither having done any good or evil, that the purpose of God according to election might stand, not of works, but of Him that calleth;) It was said unto her, The elder shall serve the younger.*
>
> Romans 9:11-12

God's plan is that our lives be ruled by the spirit, not by the soul. If we grow properly in the Spirit and in the Word, and if we have the proper leadership to guide us, God's purposes will eventually be realized in our lives, as they were in the life of Jacob. We must be ever vigilant to see that satan is not influencing our lives through the weak aspects of our soul, so that we miss the good things that God has prepared for us.

God said:

> *As it is written* [in Malachi 1:1-3], *Jacob have I loved, but Esau have I hated.*
>
> Romans 9:13

Although Jacob had his character flaws, he developed a burning desire for God. God honored that desire, molding and shaping Jacob through suffering and trial into Israel. The name *Israel* means *he shall rule as God*.

Esau, on the other hand, sold his birthright for the satisfaction of momentary appetites, without giving it a second thought. He had no real longing to be close to God. He was indifferent to the Lord, a deadly sin which has the power to destroy the greatest of men.

When we hunger for God, we get into the vine, and begin to flow in the Spirit, Father God automatically and joyfully releases to us His provisions.

I am the true vine, and My Father is the husbandman. Every branch in Me that beareth not fruit He taketh away: and every branch that beareth fruit, He purgeth it, that it may bring forth more fruit. Now ye are clean through the word which I have spoken unto you. Abide in Me, and I in you. As the branch cannot bear fruit of itself, except it abide in the vine; no more can ye, except ye abide in Me. I am the vine, ye are the branches: He that abideth in Me, and I in him, the same bringeth forth much fruit: for without Me ye can do nothing. If a man abide not in Me, he is cast forth as a branch, and is withered; and men gather them, and cast them into the fire, and they are burned. If ye abide in Me, and My words abide in you, ye shall ask what ye will, and it shall be done unto you.

John 15:1-7

As we mature in the spirit, by allowing proper oversight of our soul, one day the spirit-man will mature past the soul-man. Then the elder will serve the younger: the spirit will have dominion of the soul.

God knows what is best for us. In His love and compassion for us, as His dear children, He has designed *the porter principle* to enable us to subjugate the soul and walk in the spirit, receiving all that His hand has lovingly prepared.

Chapter 13

I Will Stand Upon My Watch

Be sober, be vigilant; because your adversary the devil, as a roaring lion, walketh about, seeking whom he may devour:

I Peter 5:8

Our God is ever-vigilant.

For the eyes of the Lord run to and fro throughout the whole earth.

II Chronicles 16:9

I will stand upon my watch....

Habakkuk 2:1

God's vigilance is warranted; for we have an enemy who never rests. He stalks about like a hungry lion searching for prey. But, as we have seen, God has given the responsibility of vigilance to men. Each of us bears some responsibility to watch.

Throughout the Old Testament, God set porters to guard His work and His people. Gideon was one of those who became a porter over Israel. When enemies came against God's people, Gideon was told how to defeat them.

And the Lord looked upon him, and said, Go in this thy might, and thou shalt save Israel from the hand of the Midianites: have not I sent thee?

Judges 6:14

When Gideon gathered his armies to battle, the Lord showed him that many of the men were not worthy to participate. He eliminated those who were fearful, lax and unprepared. Later, another division was made, so that Gideon was left with only three hundred faithful men. He took a third of them and set a watch.

So Gideon, and the hundred men that were with him, came unto the outside of the camp in the beginning of the middle watch; and they had but newly set the watch: and they blew the trumpets, and brake the pitchers that were in their hands.

Judges 7:19

We all know the story of Gideon's great victory over the Midianites. Those who are rightly aligned on God's side always win. Always!

Saul was chosen by God and appointed over Israel as its chief porter. When he went forth against the enemies of Israel, God's enemies were totally vanquished.

And it was so on the morrow, that Saul put the people in three companies; and they came into the midst of the host in the morning watch, and slew the Ammonites until the heat of the day: and it came to pass, that they which remained were scattered, so that two of them were not left together.

I Samuel 11:11

What a glorious victory! When a faithful porter is doing his job well, the foe will always be scattered.

In later years, Israel built a *watchtower in the wilderness* so that they could anticipate the approach of enemies and head them off, even before they reached the populated areas. It worked.

And when Judah came toward the watch tower in the wilderness, they looked unto the multitude, and, behold, they were dead bodies fallen to the earth, and none escaped.

II Chronicles 20:24

This need to be vigilant did not change with the times. When Nehemiah returned from captivity and rebuilt the city walls, he immediately placed porters around those walls.

And I said unto them, Let not the gates of Jerusalem be opened until the sun be hot; and while they stand by, let them shut the doors, and bar them: and appoint watches of the inhabitants of Jerusalem, every one in his watch, and every one to be over against his house.

Nehemiah 7:3

Anytime God's people or His ministry are not properly guarded, we are inviting trouble. As long as we have an enemy who never rests, we can never let down our guard either. He is always looking for a breach in the hedge.

... whoso breaketh an hedge, a serpent shall bite him.

Ecclesiastes 10:8

If the hedge of safety around God's people is, for a moment, allowed to be opened, a serpent can get through. The word translated *serpent* here not only means *a snake*; it also means *to whisper a magic spell, or an enchanter*. The word used for *biteth* means *strike with the sting, or oppress with interest on a loan*. We can be stung, oppressed, and stricken when our hedge fails and is violated.

Habakkuk was raised up as a watchman over Israel. He saw enemies that would rise against his people, even before they appeared in the land.

The burden which Habakkuk the prophet did see.

Habakkuk 1:1

In this case, the enemies were *the Chaldeans*.

For, lo, I raise up the Chaldeans, that bitter and hasty nation, which shall march through the breadth of the land, to possess the dwellingplaces that are not theirs. They are terrible and dreadful: their judgment and their dignity shall proceed of themselves.

Habakkuk 1:6-7

Habakkuk foresaw the havoc the enemies would wreak upon the land.

Their horses also are swifter than the leopards, and are more fierce than the evening wolves: and their horsemen shall spread themselves, and their horsemen shall come from far; they shall fly as the eagle that hasteth to eat. They shall come all for violence: their faces shall sup up as the east wind, and they shall gather the captivity as the sand. And they shall scoff at the kings, and the princes shall be a scorn unto them: they shall deride every strong hold; for they shall heap dust, and take it.

Habakkuk 1:8-10

I Will Stand Upon My Watch

And Habakkuk decided to do something about it.

I will stand upon my watch, and set me upon the tower, and will watch to see what he will say unto me, and what I shall answer when I am reproved.

Habakkuk 2:1

God is ever-watchful and is guarding His children. He is always ready to *show Himself* strong on our behalf. But He has also delegated responsibility to us, as porters over His heritage, to keep and nourish it. What a great privilege and responsibility! We must not fail Him.

Ezekiel was called as a set-man.

So thou, O son of man, I have set thee a watchman unto the house of Israel; therefore thou shalt hear the word at my mouth, and warn them from me.

Ezekiel 33:7

This commission to watch did not change with the dawning of the New Testament. Jesus told us to watch.

But know this, that if the goodman of the house had known in what watch the thief would come, he would have watched, and would not have suffered his house to be broken up.

Matthew 24:43

Paul warned the churches to be vigilant. To the Ephesians:

Therefore watch, and remember.

Acts 20:31

To the Corinthians:

Watch ye, stand fast in the faith, quit you like men, be strong.

I Corinthians 16:13

To the Colossians:

Continue in prayer, and watch in the same with thanksgiving;
                                            Colossians 4:2

To the Thessalonians:

Therefore let us not sleep, as do others; but let us watch and be sober.

                                            I Thessalonians 5:6

To Timothy:

But watch thou in all things.

                                            II Timothy 4:5

Peter also warned the churches to be watchful.

But the end of all things is at hand: be ye therefore sober, and watch unto prayer.

                                            I Peter 4:7

A watch must be maintained day and night, because satan never sleeps and never takes a day off. He never tires of seeking his victims.

We usually think of the responsibility of the set-man toward us. But we also have a responsibility toward the set-man. Satan knows that if he can do harm to the set-man and get by him, he can damage many others. God's set-men, therefore, are special targets of satan. He expends much energy trying to move them out of their place. Nothing is beneath him. He tries everything.

When we recognize the importance of the set-man to the entire Body, it becomes our responsibility to guard him in any way that we can and to pray for his protection. He is also a man, and must be protected from satan's influence. Nothing delights satan more than to weaken, delay, or destroy the set-man God has established.

Because the Apostle Paul was such a strong proponent of the gospel and a father to many, satan hurled at him all his venom. His trials seemed to be endless.

> *...in labours more abundant, in stripes above measure, in prisons more frequent, in deaths oft. Of the Jews five times received I forty stripes save one. Thrice was I beaten with rods, once was I stoned, thrice I suffered shipwreck, a night and a day I have been in the deep; In journeyings often, in perils of waters, in perils of robbers, in perils by mine own countrymen, in perils by the heathen, in perils in the city, in perils in the wilderness, in perils in the sea, in perils among false brethren; In weariness and painfulness, in watchings often, in hunger and thirst, in fastings often, in cold and nakedness. Beside those things that are without, that which cometh upon me daily, the care of all the churches.*
>
> II Corinthians 11:23-28

Through all of that and more, Paul remained undaunted. He did, however, request the prayers of his fellow believers (see Second Thessalonians 3:1-2).

If the Apostle Paul faced such peril daily and felt the need of the prayers of his fellow believers, can it be any different for God's apostles and five fold today? Those who are most important to the Kingdom are at greatest risk. Those are doing most are attacked most. Those who are most powerful in the presentation of the Word of God are perceived by satan as the most threatening to his kingdom. He attacks them most ferociously.

Praying always with all prayer and supplication in the Spirit, and watching thereunto with all perseverance and supplication for all saints; And for me, that utterance may be given unto me, that I may open my mouth boldly, to make known the mystery of the gospel, For which I am an ambassador in bonds: that therein I may speak boldly, as I ought to speak.

Ephesians 6:18-20

There is a clear precedent for the responsibility of the people in all this. While the priests ministered, the people kept the watch.

But let none come into the house of the Lord, save the priests, and they that minister of the Levites; they shall go in, for they are holy: but all the people shall keep the watch of the Lord.

II Chronicles 23:6

Jesus was troubled when the disciples could not watch while He was wrestling with the fate of all mankind in the darkness of Gethsemane.

And he cometh unto the disciples, and findeth them asleep, and saith unto Peter, What, could ye not watch with me one hour?

Matthew 26:40

Was it their responsibility to watch? They clearly didn't think so. They slept. Surely Jesus could take care of Himself. Yet He rebuked them for this thought and demanded to know why they had failed Him in His darkest hour.

We are commanded to pray for one another.

Confess your faults one to another, and pray one for another, that ye may be healed. The effectual fervent prayer of a righteous man availeth much.

James 5:16

Our prayers not only can restore wholeness and bring a cure, when there has been a falling aside or a failure, they also act as insulation and protection for every step that is taken. Praying for one another also helps to unite us in a bond which satan cannot easily break.

Watch and pray, that ye enter not into temptation.

Matthew 26:41

Temptation means a *putting to proof by experiment of good or experience of evil, discipline.* Continued porterage will teach you to endure and enable you to stand firm—whatever the situation. In this case, Jesus is reminding us to watch and pray for ourselves, that WE might resist temptation.

Regular prayer and Bible study, faithful church attendance, and consistent and biblical giving are all ways that we can guard against satan's attacks. When we faithfully give, God rebukes the devourer for our sakes.

Bring ye all the tithes into the storehouse, that there may be meat in mine house, and prove me now herewith, saith the Lord of hosts, if I will not open you the windows of heaven, and pour you out a blessing, that there shall not be room enough to receive it. And I will rebuke the devourer for your sakes, and he shall not destroy the fruits of your ground; neither shall your vine cast her fruit before the time in the field, saith the Lord of hosts.

Malachi 3:10-11

There is another aspect of our giving that is just as important: that of backing the commission or vision of our setmen. God honors that. Our support helps to bring unity into the Body, and we are blessed as a result.

God's final goal for His Church on the earth is for everything to be done in earth as it is in Heaven. He has structured every area of life in such a way that it can be guarded and watched over, maintained and nourished, in peace and safety. If we are willing to recognize and implement *the porter principle* in our own church, in our personal lives and in our homes, we will do much to bring about God's promised Kingdom.

Correct portering will enable Jesus to properly build His Church so that "...the gates of hell shall not prevail against it." (Matthew 16:18) Correct portering will cause us all to intimately crown Jesus as King of our life, and correct portering reveals and manifests that we "...are now returned unto the Shepherd and Bishop of our souls." (First Peter 2:25)

Recognizing this personally, I hereby renew my own commitment to stand upon my watch. And I invite you to do the same. Let *the porter principle* become the guiding principle of your life today.

Amen!